Who's In Control?

Also by Susan Isaacs

The Inner Parent
How to Talk to Children About Sex
How to Organize Your Kid's Room

WHO'S IN CONTROL?

A PARENT'S GUIDE TO DISCIPLINE

Susan Isaacs

A Perigee Book

To Murshid James S. B. Mackie

Perigee Books are published by
The Putnam Publishing Group
200 Madison Avenue New York, NY 10016

Library of Congress Cataloging-in-Publication Data

Isaacs, Susan.
  Who's in control?

  Includes index.
    1. Children—Discipline. 2. Child rearing.
I. Title.
HQ770.4.I83   1986   649'.64   85-25877
ISBN 0-399-51239-X

PRINTED IN THE UNITED STATES OF AMERICA

    3   4   5   6   7   8   9   10

Contents

Acknowledgments

I would like to thank Dr. Carol Weyland, for encouraging an ever-expanding view of growth and development during our talks together; Dr. Allan Cohen, for inspiration and support; my agent, Carol Mann, for making this project possible; and my editor at Putnam, Adrienne Ingrum, for her belief in this book.

I would also like to give special thanks to Collins Flannery, for her unstinting help with preparing my manuscripts; my parents, for encouraging my writing from childhood on; and my husband, Richard Isaacs, for his feedback and support on this book, and for being such a wonderful partner in parenting.

Introduction

JASON. At fourteen, Jason has become a discipline problem. He yells at his mother when she asks him to clean up after himself. He comes home late for dinner, and is too sullen to say where he was. His parents see that the old methods just aren't working. They don't know whether to blame Jason's behavior on teenage moods, or whether to tighten up the reins and show him who's boss.

DAVID. Anne is confused about how to handle two-year-old David. She works all day and looks forward to seeing him in the evening. But every night, as soon as they arrive home, David provokes her. He pours his blocks all over the floor or throws his clothes around, then waits for her reaction. Sometimes Anne spanks David, but it leaves her feeling angry and disappointed in herself and in him.

JENNIFER. Jennifer is having a problem in kindergarten. She hits other children when they won't do what she wants, and she frequently throws tantrums. Her teacher is concerned; her mother is surprised. She thought every five-year-old behaved that way.

Situations like these make us wonder if we should turn in our credentials as parents. Are we too lenient? Too inconsistent? Have we given our children enough attention? The truth is, effective discipline is a learning process for both parent and child. It takes time to work out and, just when things are running smoothly, our kids enter some new phase that forces us to rethink our methods. While discipline requires consistency, it also requires flexibility.

Some say bring back old-style discipline, when children knew what was coming and why, but research shows that neither "showing them who's boss" nor "letting them do as they please" is the answer. We live in times of change, and being a good parent today means something different than it did in the past. Years ago there was agreement on how children should act even if there was less concern about how they felt. It was assumed that children should be respectful, obedient, hardworking, and responsible.

In their determination to bring them up "right," parents supported one another. Developing a young person's character was a community effort. If Johnny's neighbor or the mailman saw him defacing property or smoking a cigarette, you can be sure his mother would hear about it. The people in a community felt it their duty to report any threats to Johnny's moral development. His mother may not have welcomed their advice, but it made her aware of his behavior and reinforced her disciplinary efforts. Johnny knew what was expected of him, because the same standards existed for his parents and grandparents, aunts and uncles, the librarian, his teacher, and other adults in his life.

Parents are more isolated today. Johnny's extended family may live across the country, and his neighbors may not even know his name. Adults are less likely to intervene with each other's children, and may consider such advice an intrusion on family privacy. For whatever reason, nowadays most parents have to navigate for themselves.

We also have greater hopes and expectations for our children than our ancestors did. We're concerned with their feelings, not just with making them obey, and we want to be sensitive and fair with them. We know that we can't force our values on them or make them submit to our wills—at least not for long. Today, there are too many diverse values and influences on our children for authoritarian methods to work.

We also know that children are not "little adults." They are developing and changing beings. Their minds work differently at four than at fourteen, and our approaches and techniques have to grow with them. That is why we need to look for the reasons *behind* their behavior, rather than reacting in the same way to each child. Because we want so much to do the best for them, it's difficult when problems persist to know what the right approach to solving them would be.

Jason's parents see that they need to stand firm. When they go back on a decision under pressure, Jason acts out more. His school counselor has encouraged his parents to use these insights. The counselor pointed out that, under the stress of internal change, Jason's testing is his way of making sure the world around him remains secure.

David, too, is acting out—but for attention. Unfortunately, he's getting it through unacceptable behavior. His mother is now trying some new techniques that a friend suggested. When they first come home, she sits with David before starting dinner. Then she gets him involved in an activity, and praises him for sticking to it while she cooks. Because David is used to getting attention by disrupting, she tries to ignore his negative behavior and focuses on the positive (working on the activity). Anne notices that their power struggles are decreasing.

Jennifer's mother now realizes that she can't wait for her daughter to outgrow her tantrums. Jennifer's teacher has explained that children can have temper tantrums even into their teenage years (and beyond) if they aren't helped to find more acceptable ways of reacting. Jennifer must *experience* the fact that throwing a tantrum won't get her what she wants. Having Jennifer's teacher bring up the problem gives both adults the opportunity to help Jennifer cope in new ways.

Although each of these situations is unique, the key to

approaching them is the same. And it isn't finding some magical technique, making these children see who's in control, or saying exactly the "right" thing to convince them to behave. The key is for the parents to develop awareness of how they approach discipline and how it affects their child.

This awareness is what most of us lack. We try our best to discipline, but we can't be sure how effective we are or whether our methods help or hinder our children. It is only when we gain insight through trial and error, self-examination, and discussion with others that change can take place.

Theoretical instructions fail to have lasting results because they don't take the person involved into consideration. That is why this book begins with *you,* your needs as a parent, and your attitudes and goals. It offers concrete ways to analyze your discipline style, build your skills, and overcome your weaknesses as a disciplinarian. This book should help you work in harmonious and supportive ways with others in situations requiring discipline. It will give you the basis for real change, and—most importantly—can make parenting a more satisfying task.

1

It Helps to Remember

The best place to start is with ourselves. If we can remember how we felt as children—what made us act up and how we felt when we were disciplined in different ways—our children's behavior will be less mysterious. Nobody likes to be disciplined, so we can't help but remember some negative incidents. But let's remember the positive ways that adults handled us, too.

LUCY (a single adult): "One time I had a terrible temper tantrum, and my brother, who was much older than I was, said I would have to sit in a chair until I calmed down. He sat there with me very calmly and lovingly. I threw shoes at him and continued to rant and rave, but he remained peaceful. Finally, the whole thing seemed so silly that I just stopped."

CARLA (mother of two): "One day I had been absolutely outrageous with my mother and, instead of pointing out how awful I was, she sent me out to the yard to think about my actions. I remember sitting there and feeling angry at her. Then, after a while, those feelings

11

went away. And I started thinking how much I loved her."

When we were children, we usually couldn't see beyond our own point of view. As adults we have the ability to empathize with others. We can look back and see things from our parents' perspective, and sympathize with their motivations and the stresses and strains of their lives. We can also understand our own childish behaviors, and when we ourselves become parents this can help us tune into our children.

But these memories—positive and negative—serve another function. They are clues to our own parenting styles. Those discipline episodes and the patterns of parenting we experienced are a part of the reservoir of learning that we draw on when we bring up our own children.

If we want to change our approaches to parenting, this is where we have to start. We can't change just by reading books. Change begins by understanding our experience, and integrating that insight with what we would like to do now. Most of what we have learned about parenting, though we may not be aware of it, comes from examples we grew up with. Occasionally we become aware of the ways our parents and other adults have influenced us, when we find ourselves doing the very thing or saying the very words that, as children, we vowed never to repeat when we had children of our own. But catching ourselves imitating our parents merely reflects the power of this learning process.

Psychologists refer to this assimilation of attitudes, values, and approaches to life that we observed in others as modeling. We store up the impressions of how one should approach stress or relaxation, work or play, disciplining children or nurturing them, etc. Later, when we are in a situation that our role models were in, we automatically tend to behave as they did. For this reason we may imitate those actions even when we don't want to.

"Joe vowed he would never strike a child. But when his two-year-old son would whine or act up, his automatic response was to hit him." We can see the power of modeling in problem situations, such as child abuse or alcoholism. The victim abhors his parents' actions but then goes on to repeat them. If our reservoir of learning is full of good experiences, parenting may come easily. If our experiences were more negative, and we don't want to repeat them, we have to learn new ways of responding. Here are some examples.

> DAN (father of three): "When my father spanked me, I felt totally helpless and terrified. I never understood why he did it. I guess, looking back, that I just pushed him too far. But, at the time, I felt destroyed."

Dan's insight into how he felt can help him handle his own son and daughter. He knows now that the aim isn't to make children feel helpless or to scare them, but to help them understand what's expected and experience the consequences of their actions when they don't conform to the rules. Dan has a closer relationship with his children than his father had with him, so his children already want to behave in ways that please him. This helps him see that force isn't necessary and that treating his children with respect gets the results he wants. So when he feels "pushed too far" he tries to take time out rather than dumping his frustrations on his kids.

> DAHLIA (mother of three): "I could talk my mother into anything and it always made me feel insecure because I never knew if I was right or not."

Even though she tends to let her children pressure her into saying "yes," Dahlia's memory of her own insecurity can help her now when she encounters situations that confuse her. She can reflect on how she was handled as a child. This will help cue her in to her child's needs. It even helps to be able to say to herself, "Oh, this is how my mother felt in these situations." Then she can differentiate that from what *she* feels is an appropriate way of responding. If she can stand firm when needed, real change can occur. Her mother also parented her in many positive ways, and paying attention to this one area of weakness can build Dahlia's confidence.

> ANDREA (mother of one): "I would do almost anything to keep my parents from getting angry at me. I

don't know why. They never hit me or punished me. But I lived in fear that I would displease them."

We all want to please our parents, and the wise parent lets her child know that she is loved and that her helpful behaviors are appreciated. Andrea can be sensitive to her children's desire to please her by reflecting on these memories. She might want to be especially careful not to punish her children by withdrawing love from them. This was one of the techniques her parents used which left her feeling emotionally abandoned. She can keep herself from repeating it unconsciously just by being aware that she herself could have this tendency.

Think back to your own experience. In remembering, try to focus on how you felt after an encounter involving discipline. Did you ever engage in a power struggle to see which of you—parent or child—would win in the end? Did you use the "silent treatment" and refuse to talk to your parents? Did you shout or cry? Were you angry, resentful, confused? Analyzing childhood discipline episodes step by step can also help us to look at the actual dynamics involved in those situations objectively. Reexperiencing our childhood perspective can also help us get in touch with what our real needs were in various situations. Were we asking for Mom to stop and listen? For Dad to recognize the fact that we were growing up? Remembering our past needs helps us to be more empathic with our children in the here and now.

Did the ways in which your parents handled you make you feel secure? Did you ever feel relieved when they intervened in your negative behavior? Could you depend on them to listen? To be fair? To explain? To forgive? Did they give you the chance to make amends, to apologize? Did they permit you to live with the consequences of your actions without making you feel humiliated or ashamed? Remembering can put you in touch with the positive role parental authority and structure plays in the lives of children.

Remembering can help you think about the kinds of discipline that made you feel good about yourself. Did you know what was coming to you when you broke a rule, or were you unsure how your parents would react? Were you an "angel" at times, then a troublemaker? Can you remember annoying a parent just to get attention? The adventure of trying to pull off something sneaky? The overwhelming urge to get your own way? Our children's "irrational" ways of reacting can seem less irritating when we reawaken our own childhood feelings.

Most importantly, your willingness to remember and to gain insight from your memories will help you handle discipline. We can't superimpose new techniques on old conditioned responses. But, if we are able to understand and sort out our reactions, we can make real changes—use new ideas and approach parenting with fresh energy.

Remembering doesn't have to be an isolated process. You can share memories with a spouse or a friend. Comparing notes can give you more insight into your experiences. As children, we generalized our experiences and thought everyone was going through the same things. Sharing our childhood experiences with others can dispel that myth. It also makes us aware of the reasons why as parents we all have different approaches to discipline. Remembering together makes it easier to be tolerant of the unique ways we each see things. It helps us work together.

While you look back, you could involve your children. Tell them about your childhood. Compare your parenting style with your parents'. This is a great way to discuss discipline. Without the heat of conflict, you can find out in a nonthreatening way what your children think about the whole process. Bear in mind that their perceptions will be colored by their childish desires and their level of thinking, but make use of this feedback and expand your children's perceptions. Let your kids try to imagine themselves as parents. Ask them how they would do it, what rules they would set up. This kind of talking can help you approach discipline situations with mutual understanding and harmony. Remembering can help you learn together.

Here's an exercise that may help you interpret your memories. You can do it by yourself, or with a friend or spouse. Comparing notes can add to your understanding.

1. What did the word "respect" mean in your childhood home? Is your definition different today?

In some families, a child who asks "why" is considered disrespectful. In others, children may be allowed to question freely, and the central issue of respect may revolve around respecting property and not taking each other's possessions without asking. People need to understand what respect means to *them*. You may be surprised to find that your attitude and that of your spouse or your child's teacher may differ. It helps you to be clearer about what *you* expect if you think these issues through ahead of time. What is respect? How would *you* like to see it expressed in your family?

2. Are there things a parent should never do or say?

As we mentioned, it can be disconcerting when we find ourselves doing things our parents did that we vowed never to repeat. However, those promises were made through our childhood perspectives. As adults, we may not consider taking a child's allowance away or grounding her for not calling home as a terrible punishment, even though we felt that way as children. What do we think now about what a parent should and shouldn't do?

Frequently we also observe the ways other parents discipline their children. This needn't be critical thinking. Often until we observe it in others, we don't understand why something "feels wrong" for us. When our child isn't involved, we can have the distance to evaluate a situation and think of how we would approach it. What are the reactions or approaches you have observed in yourself, your parents, or in other parents that you would like to avoid? What seems to trigger those situations? How would you avoid them?

3. What do you think about spanking?

People usually have strong feelings for or against spanking. (We will also discuss spanking in the next section.) Most "experts" oppose it. It is considered an old-fashioned, last-resort kind of disciplining. But that's why many other people favor it. They insist that it is a no-nonsense, back-to-basics approach to discipline. They say things like, "Maybe we wouldn't have so many problems with kids today if we did more spanking." What do you think? And how were your views developed?

Picture your parents' attitude toward spanking. Think

about the reasons they would give if they were arguing for or against spanking a child. If they tended not to spank, what were their reasons? Explore how those views mesh with your own. Discuss them with your spouse. Sometimes one person believes in physical punishment and the other doesn't. In those cases, compromises have to be reached.

4. What are the crucial things children need from parents?

When we try to put our thoughts about our children into words, it can sound too abstract. Most of us think instead about specific things we decide our children need, based on our experience. Love. Quality time. Intellectual stimulation. Privacy. These might be experiences we wanted in our childhood but lacked. Or they may be things that our parents gave in abundance, or that we have observed other parents giving.

Was there some quality you vowed you would always give your children? Can you put it into words? What does your spouse feel? Discussing what you feel children need, rather than just responding to each situation, can expand your abilities to work together. It helps you establish common goals that go beyond the day-to-day tactics of parent survival. You aren't just disciplining because you want a certain behavior to stop. Your goal is to stay in touch with long-range goals as parents, even when you're handling tough situations.

5. How does a "real disciplinarian" handle behavior problems?

Do you feel that you can't handle certain situations? When we link our self-esteem to our abilities to handle things "right," we can end up feeling inadequate. We're convinced that a "real" man should be able to make his child behave, or that a "good" mother should understand how her child feels. A "happy" family doesn't have children who act out, have problems at school, or blindly imitate their peers.

Many of these stereotypes come from our own parents' attitudes. Try to remember: What did your mother feel a "Mom" should be? Were there things your father felt that a man shouldn't be asked to do? What were your parents' definitions of a "real" family?

These stereotypes keep us from learning. If we think back

to our own images of our parents, we can also explore some of the labels that condition our views. Then we can begin the task of replacing those stereotypes with self-accepting, realistic goals and ideals.

6. What does it mean for a child to be "good?"

Is a good child always well-behaved? Is he someone who obeys without question, or should he be able to think for himself and follow his own conscience? What about being honest, trustworthy, responsible, kind, or considerate? Those are all "good" qualities, but how do we develop them?

Often our childhood experiences with discipline condition us to expect certain things of our own children. But those traditional ideas about being "good" may no longer fit. We don't expect preschoolers to be seen and not heard, or for children to obey without question. Yet our traditional images of what a good child is can cause us conflict. It's important to explore those images. Most of us have fantasies about "goodness" even before our children are born. Tuning into them can help us accept our children as they are. It can also make us aware that sometimes our expectations are paradoxical. We want our children to be obedient but independent, assertive but respectful, popular but above the negative influences of peers. How then can we develop realistic ideals for our children, and our expectations of them?

We will discuss helpful expectations you might have for your children in Chapter 4, but start to think about them now. How do your expectations for them compare with those your parents had for you? How are your ideas concerning your children different? Did you and your partner grow up with different expectations and values?

7. What are your views about eating? How would you have liked food to be handled as a child? What made meal times pleasant or unpleasant?

A surprising number of discipline problems revolve around eating. We feel that children *should* eat what's put before them or that they *should* clean their plates because we grew up with those expectations. Power struggles over eating can make meal times unpleasant. More importantly, childhood obesity and other eating problems are often caused by distorted expectations over food.

We can help our children have positive attitudes toward food by thinking out our expectations.

8. Is certain behavior tolerable in boys but not girls, and vice versa?

So many of our ideas about masculinity and femininity develop through the expectations our parents had for us as children. Often, they aren't even expressed in words—just reactions that paint a vivid picture of the ways an ideal boy or girl should be. Maybe we didn't fit the ideal. Maybe we are still trying to. But all our good intentions to be liberated parents begin with understanding the attitudes we grew up with.

What did your parents think about being male or female? How do those ideas mesh with current attitudes about men and women? How do they connect with your feelings about what you want for your children?

9. When should a parent discuss sex with a child?

Sometimes we profess certain beliefs about sexuality and sex education and then fail to act accordingly. This difficult subject is made even more difficult when we aren't really aware of how our role models behaved with us. Discipline problems relating to sexuality in the teen years can result at least in part from lack of communication. But it's hard to communicate when we aren't sure what we believe, when we should talk, or what limits we need to set.

What were your parents' attitudes toward sexuality? How did they approach communication? What did they think about your budding sexuality? Were sexual matters ever a discipline issue?

Think about how these attitudes and the feelings you had about them as you were growing up mesh with what you want for your child today.

10. What is the best thing for me to do when I don't know how to handle a problem with my child?

How do you view yourself as a problem-solver? How did your parents solve new problems? Did they ask their own parents or relatives for advice? Did they follow Dr. Spock, discuss matters with neighbors and friends? Did they parent by instinct?

Times have changed, but our ideas about how to handle problems may not have changed with them. We may still feel that people who go outside the family for help are "failures," or that only "experts" have the answers. We may be embarrassed to talk about our lives with others or maybe we always look to others for advice.

Most of us fall somewhere between these extremes, but they illustrate how diverse problem-solving can be. Our ability to solve the big and little challenges that occur every day is what makes us feel "in control." How do you meet challenges? Where are your resources? Who are your main sources of support?

As new parents, we may fantasize about a stress-free family life that never materializes. When we feel strained and overwhelmed, we might take to heart what Dr. Scott Peck, psychologist and author of the bestselling *The Road Less Traveled* (Simon and Schuster, New York, 1978) has said about solving problems:

> Problems call forth our wisdom; indeed they create our courage and wisdom. It is only because of problems that we grow mentally and spiritually. When we desire to encourage the growth of the human spirit, we challenge and encourage the human capacity to solve problems, just as in school we deliberately set problems for our children to solve. . . . It is for this reason that wise people learn not to dread but actually to welcome problems . . .

Discuss your views of problem-solving with your spouse or a friend. When we actually think about our characteristic ways of solving problems—rather than just trying to plough through difficult issues—we open ourselves to new approaches, new resources, new ways of supporting each other.

Now that we have dipped back into our pasts and analyzed some of the ways they affect the present, let's think about the future. What do we know about the long-range effects of different approaches to discipline? Thinking about our hopes for ourselves and our children can help us have a better perspective on discipline in the present.

2

The Effects of Discipline

We know that people discipline in different ways. We also know that discipline affects more than a child's immediate behavior. Discipline has traditionally been viewed as a form of character development in our culture, and even today people tend to agree—whatever their approach—that the way a parent disciplines will affect the kind of person a child becomes. But what are those effects? Does anyone really know?

Arliss and Jim let their kids decide most things for themselves. Visitors often complain that their home is dominated by the children, who interrupt or argue with each other as if guests weren't there. There is no sense that adults should be accorded respect or even a little privacy. But Arliss and Jim are comfortable with their kids and with their own easygoing approach. They feel "sorry" for parents who are more heavy-handed and seem alienated from their children. Arliss and Jim are confident that their children will grow up to be independent, and therefore not feel compelled to rebel against authority. In reality, they've never had any authority at home to rebel against.

Dawn, a single parent, treats her kids like little adults. If she says "jump" she wants them to jump *now*—not when they're good and ready. Her children don't dominate the home. But even though they are obedient, they often feel angry at her arbitrariness. They wouldn't dare talk back to her, though they frequently complain to other children and to their father about how uptight and "mean" their mother is. They feel she doesn't listen to their point of view or consider their feelings. Dawn considers this just part of being a parent: She doesn't enjoy playing the heavy, but as a single parent and the breadwinner, she feels she must be in control and "strong." She can't be around her kids as much as she would like and feels that if they don't respect her authority, she can't be effective.

Although these parents approach their children in different ways, their behavior is typical of particular styles of discipline, reflecting our expectations for ourselves and our children. Arliss and Jim have a permissive style, whereas Dawn is power-oriented. People often don't know what their style is, and may be even less aware of its effects. We can be so absorbed in the everyday decisions of whether Johnny should be allowed to see that movie or go downtown with his friends that we don't step back to see the *patterns* in our behavior. We may get little feedback from others about our style of parenting, and advice from well-meaning relatives about how we should do things differently may not be as helpful as it is intended to be.

Analyzing our style can motivate us to change. We may worry that we are too strict or permissive, but comparing our approaches with the styles outlined below can provide direct feedback. We must remember that our perceptions may not correspond with the way others see us. And, due to extensive research over the last decades documenting the long-term effects of particular discipline styles, we don't need to guess what the effects of certain approaches to discipline might be—the evidence is there. Using this research can help us understand our own approaches, and analyze whether or not they fit our long-term goals as parents.

POWER-ORIENTED STYLE OF DISCIPLINE

"Do it because I say so."

"Stop it right now if you don't want a spanking."

"Don't you dare question what I say. Just remember, I'm the parent here."

Power-oriented discipline has had long-standing popularity. Power-oriented parents get children to do what they want by exerting control. Threatening, yelling, commanding, and hitting are all tactics of power-oriented discipline, because these parents attempt to shape the child's behavior on the basis of their "greater" strength. The traditional goal of power-oriented discipline was to break the child's will. Power-oriented parents today are more apt to talk in terms of keeping a child "in line" or "showing him who's boss."

This form of discipline has been such an integral part of our heritage that it has been accepted in some communities as the only legitimate form of discipline. If we have never known any other approach, it can be hard to think of it as just another style. But it is merely one kind of discipline, not the "only" way.

Most parents use power techniques at one time or another. Children of parents who use them *most* of the time often have particular behavior patterns. These children tend to be:

- power-oriented with their peers. They try to get what they want through aggression, and settle conflicts by fighting.
- less open to reasoning. Research shows that when parents have not used reasoning as a part of discipline, children tend not to respond when it is introduced.
- less considerate of other people. Children whose parents are power-oriented tend to be less concerned with others' feelings.
- more discontent, withdrawn, and distrustful of people than other children.
- more independent than children of permissive parents.

PERMISSIVE STYLE OF DISCIPLINE

"If that's what you want to do, go ahead."

"Don't come running to me if you get hurt. Just remember, it's your decision."

Unlike power-oriented parents, permissive parents often are not aware that what they're doing is a form of discipline. Most power-oriented parents brag about being strict and in control, but permissive parents typically have less sense of what their style is. They may adopt a noncontrolling stance for many reasons: They want to be "pals" with their children; they don't like disciplining; their own parents were "too strict"; their own parents were permissive; they are busy or otherwise distracted in their own lives; they believe children need a lot of freedom and that adults and children should be equals.

Whatever the reason, permissive parents tend to have certain things in common. They have low expectations for their children. They accept immature or regressive behavior. They exercise little control over their child's behavior, and seldom play the role of the authority. They may ignore a child's aggressive tendencies (demandingness, name-calling, or hitting) because they are convinced the child can't control those impulses or because they think that type of self-expression is psychologically healthy. They trust that their child will eventually evolve to more mature behavior. All in all, they make few interventions to help the child behave appropriately. They trust that he will grow more happily on his own.

Children whose parents have a permissive orientation tend to be:

- less self-reliant and independent than children of power-oriented parents or authoritative parents
- less able to control their own impulses
- more dependent on adults
- least responsible toward their peers
- close to their parents, if the relationship is warm and supportive

AUTHORITATIVE STYLE OF DISCIPLINE

"When you take someone's toy, it makes them angry. If you don't give it back, I'll have to give it back for you."

"I get worried when you're late and don't call. Next time you forget, you won't be allowed to stay after school for baseball practice for three days."

Psychologists have identified a third discipline style, which does not use power to get children to behave but which does actively shape behavior. Psychologists have called it authoritative discipline. Authoritative disciplinarians have high expectations for children, but they don't command them. They try to motivate them and they applaud their children's efforts to behave positively. Authoritative disciplinarians are both nurturing and firm. They set limits and stick by them, explaining ahead of time the reasons for rules and the consequences that will occur if rules are broken. They also try to follow through consistently on what they say.

Children of authoritative parents tend to be:

- more self-confident than children of power-oriented or permissive parents
- more considerate of other children, according to their teachers and peers
- the most independent and self-reliant of all three groups of children
- close to their parents
- more capable of reasoning on their own

If you don't know which of these categories you fall into, don't worry. People tend to be power-oriented in some situations, permissive in others. However, looking at these styles gives us a picture of the long-range effects of discipline. It reminds us that it isn't the way we handle an isolated incident that makes a difference in children's lives but the typical, repeated ways we act that affect them most profoundly. Recognizing our overall patterns of discipline will give us a structure for change, and take away our guilt for

those occasions when we have reacted in ways we don't like.
We can get a new sense of patterns in our behavior.

But how can we change? What if we are permissive and
feel frustrated at putting up with bad behavior? What if we
don't really like yelling at our children or threatening them
when they get on our nerves? Does handling situations in
new ways require a big investment of time and energy? In
the next section, we will learn how gradually to effect the
changes you want to make in your style and attitude.

Here's an exercise that can help you think about discipline styles.

1. How would you characterize your parents' styles of
disciplining? Were they mixtures of these three styles—
power-oriented about some things, permissive about
others, or authoritative?

2. Did your mother's style differ from your father's?
Did those differences cause conflict between them and
confusion for you? What were their parents like when it
came to disciplining?

3. How is your style like either or both of your parents'? What words would you use to describe it? How is
it different?

4. Think about other parents you know. Can you iden-
tify any power-oriented parents among your friends?
Permissive ones? Authoritative ones?

3

Building Discipline Skills

Trying to change the way we discipline young children and adolescents can seem like a Herculean task. That's because we often don't know where to start and assume we must change everything all at once. It wouldn't be effective to reorganize our house by tearing everything apart at once—we need to start in one room, or even one closet, and move to another in an orderly way—we must tackle the problem bit by bit.

To learn to do anything, we need to break it into parts. That's how we make it manageable. Recipes have steps. Gardening has prescribed procedures. Discipline can be made easier, too. Because we have identified authoritative discipline as the style with the most beneficial effects for children, we have divided it into actual skills or abilities that we can aim for and work on one at a time. To be effective, discipline requires five important skills:

- thinking ahead
- motivating
- communicating clearly
- following through
- working with others

Recognizing these skills can help us to understand how to discipline in more effective ways. Discipline may seem like a win-or-lose proposition: either we know how to do it, or we don't. But that's not the case. We all have strengths and weaknesses when it comes to these abilities. The trouble is, most of us don't know what our strengths and weaknesses are. Without feedback or introspection, we are likely to fall into a rut. We may feel that communicating with our child is the key, when what we really need to work on is giving him more effective consequences. Without understanding the importance of each of these disciplinary abilities, we might try only one tactic again and again—with little effect.

If we hired a child development specialist to come into our homes and observe us for a few days, he or she could probably point out our strengths and weaknesses rather easily. "You're great at motivating your child when things are going well between you. But when there's a problem, you need to communicate what you want from him more clearly. You tend to repeat yourself, and often he isn't paying attention."

But you don't need to hire an expensive consultant. You can diagnose your own strengths and weaknesses by exploring the five skills discussed in this chapter and whether or not they are part of your own approach to discipline on a daily basis. This should be an encouraging process: Don't just look at the things you *don't* do, look at the positive efforts you already make. Pay attention to the ways you usually react, not the occasional lapses when you and your child are overly tired or burdened.

After a first reading, consider each skill carefully with one or two discipline problems that you want to analyze in mind. Think about the attention and effort you have put into those skills. Have you tended to emphasize one more than another? Once you have a clear picture of these skills and how they relate to your discipline style, you can focus on the ones you want to work on. This is a way to make realistic change—step by step. As we and our children grow, we may need to concentrate on different skills, so this is a section we may want to read both now and later, as we are presented with new challenges. That way we can also keep track of the positive ways we have changed.

Here are the five skills required of authoritative disciplinarians, and some nuts-and-bolts suggestions for achieving them.

THE ABILITY TO THINK AHEAD

ANN (mother of three): "Over the years, I have discovered the incredible value of thinking ahead. When my teenager hasn't called and is coming home late, or when my children have fallen into some pattern that is irritating, I think things out carefully. I plan a consequence ahead of time for that child who is late. I think out a plan to motivate my kids to get out of that negative behavior. I set up new rules. I still get upset, but it's the thinking ahead that makes me able to handle things calmly and in a way that makes them listen and respond positively. When I don't do it, things turn into an argument much more easily."

Do you think about recurring problems with your child, and plan strategies for handling them? Have you worked out rules with her? Do you anticipate situations you will be going into and try to prepare your child if they may be hard for him to deal with? Do you try to adjust your child's physical environment to minimize problems with a sibling or enhance playtime with other children?

The ability to anticipate is an important part of discipline. Often we don't think of it as a skill. We may concentrate more on carrying out this or that technique instead of thinking and planning. But, the ability to think ahead can make the difference between feeling in control and feeling overwhelmed. As in any activity, thinking ahead helps us to plan, organize, and feel prepared.

When we observe parents we admire disciplining, it may seem spontaneous. Aren't we supposed to know how to react in any situation? No. In reality, the people who have learned to be authoritative disciplinarians are those who have thought beforehand about how they will handle situations when they are *not* disciplining. That way, they develop an organized approach and aren't always thrown off guard. Thinking ahead is the first step in discipline, and here are some suggestions for achieving this skill.

Anticipate Situations

Lydia was driving her five-year-old son to the grocery store.
  "I want candy."
  "Not today, Donny."
  "I want *candy*."
  "No, Donny. You'll ruin your dinner."
  "CANDY!!"
Donny threw a tantrum and refused to get out of his car seat when they arrived at the store.

If Lydia had anticipated Donny's demand, she might have been able to prevent the frustration and grief of a tantrum. She might have talked to Donny about what they were going to buy that day, interested him in a healthier "treat," or distracted him by their surroundings on the way to the store. It's not that she mishandled the situation—her only problem was that she didn't anticipate.

Frustrating interactions such as this one can result when we: (1) don't set up the situation ahead of time to make it more harmonious; (2) don't coordinate with spouses or other adults who are involved; (3) make a hasty decision; or (4) get surprised or confused in the midst of a situation.

Avoid Reactions that Make Children Resentful

If we anticipate that Susie will run in with mud all over her shoes, or that Bill will forget to call, we can plan ahead to prevent an unfortunate confrontation. A cardboard sign outside the door could remind Susie to take care of her dirty shoes. When Bill comes home, we can greet him in a way that may make him *want* to call the next time: "Bill, I was worried. I guess I didn't make it clear enough how important it is to call. How can I help you to remember next time?" These are more effective than angry responses: "Why don't you ever wipe your feet, Susie?" "Bill, how many times have I told you to call?"

Of course there will always be surprises, but the more frequently and thoroughly we think through issues—lateness, messiness, breaking rules—the more we can respond positively and effectively to the unexpected.

Work on the Most Troublesome Behaviors

When discipline is a problem, everything seems wrong. Dana's parents are upset because she talks on the phone too long, drops her clothes all over the house, plays loud music, and leaves her homework until the last minute. However, blasting Dana with all those complaints overwhelms both Dana and her parents. When they nag her about all the things she is doing wrong, she tunes them out.

Just as adults can only effectively work on one or two weaknesses at a time, we need to limit what we expect of our children. Dana's parents must choose specific issues to work on, and not more than one or two at a time. If they decide that Dana's messiness will be the focus, they should agree what the consequence of it will be, and let Dana know what they expect. ("We want you to stop cluttering the house with your clothes. If we find them around when we come home next time, we'll put them in a box and hold them for a week.") This straightforward approach can reduce anger on both sides.

It also prevents us from making threats that we are not prepared to carry out. "If I find your clothes on the floor one more time, I'm going to throw them out!" Or, "I'll keep you from watching TV for one week!" When we don't think ahead, we make futile threats. Threats can also encourage the very behavior we're trying to diminish, because children may want to see if we will carry them out and test us until we do. Parents must be able to live with the threats they make.

MIKE (father of two): "We think a lot about what we are going to work on and what the consequences will be. Sometimes we're not able to live with a consequence, and then it doesn't work. For instance, if we had to restrict the girls from watching TV in the morning, we'd never be ready on time. So we try to predict what will work ahead of time."

Consider the Consequences

Thinking about annoying behaviors and what reasonable consequences for them should be can help us to avoid excessive punishment or other ineffective reactions. When we don't anticipate, we usually respond by yelling, spanking, blaming, or feeling confused—automatic, negative responses.

Sherry learned that when she overreacted, her children would try to hide things from her. They were afraid of what she would do. She learned to take time out before she reacted. What were the important issues, she would ask herself. Was what had happened really so bad? How could she help her child most?

Having stated consequences ahead of time ("You'll have to leave the table if this continues"; "If you want to be loud, you'll have to do it in your room") gives us control over ourselves and the situation. If you establish behavioral rules, you won't have to cope on a crisis-by-crisis basis. This saves time and energy, and makes it possible for a child to gear his actions to expectations. These might include no eating away from the table, no running in the house, no breakfast after 8:00 A.M., no record playing between 7:00 and 9:00 A.M.

Once rules have been set and their consequences followed through, children don't test parental limits as hard. They learn it's a waste of time.

Take Time to Make Decisions

"Can I go to the show with Tommy, please, Mom?" "Can I go to the dance?" "Can I ride my new bike to the store?" "Can I fingerpaint this morning?"

Often we feel pressured to answer children immediately. But if we take time out, even just five minutes, we can make a better decision. We may need more information, or may want to check the matter out with our spouse or another parent. Sometimes we have to look over our schedules. We owe it to our children to make reasonable decisions. Under pressure, we may get angry and refuse a request for no reason, or give in to a request that we later regret.

Nancy set up a rule that her children were not allowed to pressure her for a decision. Once they asked to do something, they had to back off while she thought about it for a while. Otherwise the answer would automatically be "No."

Conclusion

Thinking ahead doesn't mean that you will be able to anticipate or avoid every crisis. It doesn't mean that you will have all the answers or that everything you try will work. It doesn't guarantee that you won't lose your temper or act in ways you later regret. But it does give you a precious opportunity. When you think ahead, which really means evaluating how you handled situations in the past and how you want to handle them in the future, you can do more than just react. And taking time to think when situations do arise will equip you with a degree of detachment—enough to act with insight.

No one can think in the heat of an argument, or when a child is whining or crying, or when siblings are about to do each other in. But when we have already thought things out, we may not be as confused by events and can more likely handle them with wisdom.

If you have always wanted to stay just one tiny step ahead of your child, thinking ahead is the key.

THE ABILITY TO MOTIVATE

> DIANE (mother of two): "I don't want to have to nag my child to help. I want him to *want* to be a responsible person. I want him to care. I won't always be there to force him to do the things he should."

Can you make working together fun? Has praise ever motivated your child toward a different way of behaving? Have you ever used incentives to help your child give up an irritating habit? Do you consciously pay attention to your child's positive efforts?

Many people don't think of motivating as an aspect of discipline. Rather they think of discipline as related to punishment and to convincing children to "behave." But motivating a child in positive ways is the most important component of discipline. If our children don't want to please us, if they have no interest in behaving positively, discipline will be an uphill battle. When our lives are a series of power struggles, neither we nor they will come out the winner.

Motivating a child is a process of building the positive: building our positive relationship; building the child's positive self-image; and building incentives for behaving positively in the structure of everyday life.

When we talk about consistency in discipline, we usually mean following through on what we say. But we need to be consistent in being good motivators, too. We need to inspire the best in our children and convince them that they are successfully working on becoming the kind of people we want them to be—kind, helpful, honest, considerate, and responsible.

If you have to nag your child to get him to do what's expected, if he gets attention primarily for negative behavior, or if you would like him to *want* to change a way of behaving, effective motivation can make a dramatic difference.

Here are some ways to motivate a child's best behavior.

Focus on the Positive

DANIELLE (ten-year-old): "When I'm in my piano lesson and my teacher says she thinks I've improved or she likes what I'm doing, it helps me to play better for that hour. If she says I'm not doing well, I get really nervous and I can hardly play at all. She usually says I'm doing well, though."

The majority of time spent with children should make them feel good about themselves. If we spend a lot of time correcting them, our focus on negative behavior may become a habit. And children can learn to provoke adults to unpleasant reactions, just to get attention.

A preschool teacher comments:

"I had a very difficult child in my class who was used to provoking her parents. This was obvious in morning circle because she would disrupt everything and then look directly at me with a mischievous smile. If I reacted with anger or tried to correct her verbally, she would do it more. But I forced myself to ignore those behaviors and to praise her every time she was quiet in circle. Within several months her behavior was transformed."

We usually think of discipline as the means to correcting or punishing "bad" behavior. However, attention focused for positive efforts or accomplishments has far greater results than any other form of discipline. When we want to encourage more positive behavior, thinking about motivating our child is our most valuable resource.

One mother says, "I've noticed a big difference in my daughter's behavior over the last year. She sees herself as a helpful person. But that's because we started expressing our appreciation *whenever* she offered help. That praise inspired her to help more often and to feel confident about helping."

Spend Time Together

One of the most helpful things parents can do for their children is to spend time with them. We don't usually think of that as being a part of discipline, but it's crucial. When children know that they can count on us to give them our undivided attention, many problems just melt away. Not only do children feel secure when they have attention, but spending time together actually inspires good behavior.

MAY (mother of three): "When I take my ten-year-old daughter out away from the rest of the family just for a short time, and eat with her or go shopping, I'm always amazed by the results. When we come home, discipline issues about her helping or getting mad seem to evaporate. She actually wants to be helpful. When I put it off for a while and things are hard between us, I start thinking I have to get tough on her. It never works. Then we have a special time together, and I think, Why don't I do this more often? The results are miraculous."

Genuine Praise

It's helpful to praise children's efforts, but all forms of praise do not have this effect. Stop and think how you feel when someone says, "You're looking better today." You may wonder just how awful you looked yesterday, or what it is about you that's different and praiseworthy today.

Johnny is confused by his grandmother's vague praise. When she says he's a "good" boy, he doesn't know what she means. Is he "bad" at other times? Johnny cannot grasp what exactly his grandmother is appreciating about him, therefore he doesn't know how to get a positive response from her again.

Praise that genuinely makes us feel appreciated usually refers to specific aspects of our behavior or appearance, and is phrased in terms of the speaker's feelings. Faint praise can foster resentment. A child may feel we are judging him or that his efforts rarely measure up.

Helpful Praise	*Faint Praise*
I love your hair that length.	Your hair sure looks better.
I really appreciate all the time you spent on this project.	You can be a good worker when you try.
I love the way you rearranged your room.	Your room looks a lot better.

Specific praise lets your child know exactly what is appreciated, and helps to reinforce his or her behavior.

Offer Choices

When children are encouraged to make choices, it shows them their parents have trust in their good judgment. Authoritative parents encourage their children to make choices they are capable of making and permit them to learn from the consequences. Power-oriented parents often feel they must make all the decisions, without realizing that children benefit from decision-making.

Ali, for example, earns her own money babysitting and her mother lets her decide how she wants to spend it. But when Ali makes a bad purchase, her mother doesn't "rescue" her by giving her more money. This way, Ali is learning to plan and budget on her own.

A two-year-old can probably decide between outfits he wants to wear; a four-year-old can decide who to invite over and what game she wants to play. When we don't trust children to make some independent decisions and experience the results of them, they will feel inadequate or forced into decisions. On the other hand, when parents go too far to the other extreme and make no decisions or rules at all—especially with adolescents—choices can be overwhelming and self-defeating. It's up to parents to judge their children's capacity to choose for themselves.

Think About Rewards

Some parents balk at the idea of rewards because they think good behavior should be its own reward. However, just as some businesses offer rewards for high productivity and increased sales, incentives at home may motivate good behavior and add to the spirit of an activity.

Ceci was slow getting into bed so her parents set up a two-week system of rewards. She got a dime every evening that she didn't dawdle. Ceci became speedy and kept up the habit, even when the two-week reward period ended.

The purpose of incentives is to motivate children to change. For example, you and your son could talk about how often he makes his bed and does his chores each week, and then have him keep track of his performance during the next week. The reward for better performance might be an ice cream sundae, a raise in allowance, a movie, or time at a video game parlor—whatever motivates *him*. Incentives help a child see how he is improving.

Remember, though, there is a crucial difference between rewards and bribes. For example, when Jay whines in the supermarket, his mother buys a package of cookies to keep him quiet. That is a bribe. Incentives, on the other hand, provide *goals* that children can work toward. An incentive would be earning a day at an amusement park by doing chores without complaining and on time for a month. Doing the chores that way for a month will help set up a positive pattern, so rewards may not be necessary in the future. When habits take hold, you can set new goals and new rewards.

Incentive systems are especially helpful for children who have trouble with a particular skill, whether it is toilet training, doing chores, finishing homework on time, or cleaning up. But it's the child's consistent *efforts* that should be rewarded, not the results. Therefore, paying or rewarding children for good grades may be inappropriate. The reward should go for the studying and work the child did.

Here is an example of a Star Chart that parents might occasionally use to improve a child's efforts in some area. This chart can give Amy direct feedback and positive reinforcement for her efforts in different areas. School-age children especially like to see concrete evidence of their achievements, and the chart itself acts as an incentive—especially when the child is working toward a reward.

Communicate Positive Attitudes

How would you describe your child? Trustworthy? Responsible? Immature? Capable? You would be surprised how important your own perception is. Children unconsciously live up to their parents' image of them.

Parents who see their children as trustworthy tend to have trustworthy children. It makes sense: Parents who believe their children are responsible give them more opportunities to develop a personal sense of responsibility. Those who distrust their children will probably limit their opportunities for growth by not providing them with situations that demand responsibility.

STAR CHART

For: Amy Brown   **September 21–27**

	MON	TUES	WED	THUR	FRI	SAT	SUN
1. Pick up your things.							
2. Feed the dog.							
3. Come home on time.							
4. Make your bed.							
5. Brush your teeth.							
6. Go to bed on time.							
7. Do two extra things you aren't asked to.							

The first words Tommy's mother would greet him with when he was late were a suspicious "And where have you been?" Then Tommy would become sullen, and they wouldn't talk for the rest of the evening. Tommy always felt his mother didn't trust him.

The more a child learns that he is worthy of trust, the greater his own sense of well-being and confidence.

Conclusion

Our ability to encourage children can help them in every area of life. Furthermore, the focus on encouragement and motivation helps us as parents. Letting our children *choose* to behave in kind, responsible, considerate ways puts us in touch with a deeper reality than the typical approach to discipline. The point isn't to control or coerce. It is more important to inspire children to their highest ideals and behaviors, to equip them to be good decisionmakers and independent thinkers, and to treat them as we would have them behave toward others.

Where does the desire to consider others and act in positive ways come from? Research shows that parents who value kindness and behave in considerate ways with their children—even while disciplining—have children who are regarded by their peers as being kind and considerate. Therefore motivation can't be just something we talk about. We must put it into practice. It has to do with who we are and how we relate in loving ways to our children and others.

THE ABILITY TO COMMUNICATE

> PAT (mother of two): "I make my fourteen-year-old repeat back what the arrangements are when he's going out. I've learned from experience that all kinds of mixups occur if I'm not sure he's heard me, so we go over it. It saves so much energy and prevents unpleasant hassles when I know the communication is clear."

Do you get your child's attention before you give directions or explain what you want? Do you describe the behavior you want rather than just saying "Stop it"? Do you set aside time to talk about a problem with your child? Do you have family meetings?

Sometimes it seems as if our children need hearing aids. Other times, when we don't want them to hear, their ability to decipher our words seems quite acute. Living as a family, we tune out certain things and pick up on others. Ineffective communication can waste lots of time and energy; a child may not really hear what his parent is saying, or a parent doesn't really listen to his child. Often this is because not enough time is allotted for talking at quiet moments, when discipline *isn't* occurring.

The ability to communicate clearly can keep discipline from exhausting us and making us feel ineffective. We have to learn to hear and be heard, to build up our skills at talking with our children. If you have to repeat instructions more than once, if your child doesn't look up from the TV when you speak, or if most of what you say has to do with correcting your child, consider working on communication.

Here are some ways to improve it.

Analyze Communication Problems

> BILL (father of one): "I had a habit of saying general things like 'Aaron, please pick up your stuff, OK?' He'd say 'Huh?' at least once. I'd repeat myself, and then he'd ignore me. It took a lot of practice for me to be able to think out exactly what I wanted him to do, get his attention by calling his name or touching his arm, and then say only once, 'Aaron, I want you to please pick up your toys right now.'"

Many parents find that their children don't even hear what they're saying, so they feel defeated from the start. We assume that our children understand our wishes and are purposely ignoring us. Signs that communication is not working include:

- We repeat ourselves often
- Our children do not respond
- Negative behavior continues in spite of warnings
- Our children insist they didn't hear or understand us

This can be due to the following situations:

1. We don't express what we want in simple, positive terms ("I need you to turn off the TV now"). Instead we frame things in negative or incriminating ways ("Would you

turn that thing off?" or "How many times have I told you not to watch TV while you're studying?").

2. We are uncertain how children will react to requests, so we make them in a wishy-washy or unclear way ("Can't you stop making noise?").

3. We think that convincing a child that we are right will make him want to listen ("I can't believe you're doing that after I warned you").

4. We compete with other distractions for a child's attention instead of changing the atmosphere to aid communication ("Can't you look up from the TV?").

5. We don't ask for a child's participation in the conversation ("I said do it now").

Consider how you approach communication, and how the above guidelines might help.

Set Up a Relaxed Atmosphere

Matt and his mother always have a snack together after school. This is a special time for them to be alone, without the pressure to get anything done. While they eat Matt inevitably talks about his day in a casual way. His mother doesn't pry into his affairs, but while they are eating his concerns seem to come out naturally.

Just as you wouldn't ask your husband or wife to discuss financial affairs the moment he or she walks in the door exhausted from work, you can't expect children to be receptive to discussing problems when they have just gotten in from school or play, or when they feel vulnerable and upset. Unless your concern is urgent, choose a relaxed time and place. Be sure you have their attention and that they are not distracted by other people or activities. If the problem is a long-range one, like watching too much TV or leaving clothes around, approach your children when you can talk alone and at length. Don't start a critical discussion at 8:55 when bedtime is at 9:00.

Choosing a relaxed atmosphere allows better communication. It helps when we plan situations that encourage our children to share with us.

State Your Wishes

When Janice said, "You guys have really messed up this living room and you should clean it up," nothing happened. But when she said, "I need you to clean up the living room now so that I can have friends over," she got results.

Take responsibility for your feelings rather than blaming others.

Blaming Statements	*"I" Statements*
You never clean up.	I need you to clean up before dinner.
Can't anyone ever help me?	I need you to carry in the groceries.
You never do what I say.	I need more help around the house.
What are you so inconsiderate?	I need people to be quiet when I'm resting.
Don't bother me now.	I need to be alone now.

Don't Ask Incriminating Questions

Anne still remembers how she felt as a child when her mother asked, "Are you playing doctor again?" She was so ashamed she wanted to hide. The question itself made her feel that this was something no nice girl would do. She couldn't even bring herself to answer.

One of the dangers of negative communication is that our children learn not to hear us at all. Why should they want to listen when we make statements or questions that blame them?

Questions That Make Children Defensive	*"I" Message*
Why did you do that?	I need you to stop.
Why didn't you come when I called you?	I need you to come as soon as I call.
Why do you talk to me like that?	I need you to talk to me in a respectful way.

Questions That Make Children Defensive	*"I" Message*
Why are you being such a brat?	I need you to calm down.
Why didn't you stop when I told you?	I need you to put your things down as soon as I tell you.
Where have you been all this time?	I was expecting you at 5 o'clock.

Questions that force people to explain their actions, motivations, or reasoning usually put them on the defensive, thereby angering them. Mary knows when she's been asking her teenage son to explain too many details. He usually says, "Mom, you're really starting to get on my case." Our communication goal is to encourage discussion and problem-solving. If, instead of insisting that children explain the behaviors that we dislike we concentrate on explaining our needs or the behavior that we do desire, we will improve our communication.

Give Clear Messages

Cindy likes to complain a lot: She's so tired, she can hardly move; her stomach hurts. These complaints usually occur right before she is supposed to do her chores. Her mother has learned to say, "I'm sorry you're not feeling up to par, but I need you to do your chores now. Why don't you rest afterwards?"

Acknowledge that you understand your children's feelings, but don't get sidetracked. Listen to them express their feelings, but state your expectations:

"I understand that you don't feel like mowing the lawn, **but it needs to be done this afternoon.**"

"I know you don't want to stop watching TV right now, **but I want you to finish the dishes.**"

"I know you don't want to hang up, **but I need to use the phone.**"

"I know you don't want to put on your coat, **but I'm going to wait right here by the door until you do.**"

The above statements acknowledge a child's feelings, but still get your point across. It's important to listen to expressions of unfairness or anger. But there is a fine line between being a sensitive, effective parent and one who is such a good "listener" that she lets her own message go unspoken.

For example, ten-year-old Joan doesn't want to start her homework. There is a special TV program on at 8:00. If Joan's mother plays the role of "listener," she may spend so much time listening to Joan's arguments about why she should be able to watch TV that the issue may never get resolved. It would be more effective to set another time for them to discuss TV watching and focus on the problem of homework.

Making our immediate wishes known requires a direct approach. The goal is to concentrate on sending a clear message, while still acknowledging a child's underlying feelings. Joan's mother might say: "I know it's hard to do your homework when there's a special show on, but homework comes first." No argument.

Don't Judge or Criticize

When parents make and keep appointments to discuss issues, children can be more cooperative. Joan's mother should follow through on her commitment to discuss TV watching.

Sometimes, however, parents lead children into a kind of trap. They say they want to hear their children's complaints, but if those complaints make parents angry and defensive, they may find it hard to listen. They defend or justify their behavior, or dictate to their children how and what they should feel.

Sean wanted a time to talk about his math problems. But when he started describing some of the assignments he hadn't turned in, all he got was a lecture about his irresponsibility. If you're going to have a real discussion, you need to listen and try to help children articulate their feelings.

BETH (mother of three): "My daughter has a hard time getting along with her father (my ex-husband). At first it would be hard to listen to her feelings about him without correcting her or telling her how to solve her problems. But then I realized she desperately needed someone who could just sit and listen, so that's what I learned to do."

Conclusion

The ability to communicate in ways that satisfy us and our children is the strand that connects us with them as we *both* grow and change. We will inevitably have conflicts. We will feel different things and have different ideas about how things should be. But if we can still communicate—if we value the activity of sharing in spite of conflict—our relationships will continue in positive ways.

Nurture communication. Sacrifice other activities to make time for it. Schedule it. Listen even when you don't want to. Have faith in the things you want to say to your children, even if it's hard to find the right words.

Your children may not always hear what you are saying, but they will *feel* the efforts you make and they can't help but respond to your motivation to help them.

FOLLOWING THROUGH

MIKE (father of two): "I find if I don't follow through appropriately and carry out the consequence, it can end up badly. I get mad, they get mad because they didn't understand that I really meant what I said, and it turns into a power struggle. It's easier just to follow through from the start."

Do you explain ahead of time what the consequences will be if your child continues a certain behavior? Do you follow through the *first* time your child carries on an activity you've asked her to stop? Do you carry out consequences for breaking rules in a matter-of-fact way rather than punitively? Can you keep from being intimidated by your child and giving in?

Following through means we do what we say. If we promised a reward for being quiet the whole ride, we don't put off giving it until it's convenient. If we warned our child that we would take him out of the restaurant if he continued whining, we don't wait until we are through eating and the bill is paid.

Following through means we do what we say but without making our child feel bad. (The purpose of punishing is to inflict emotional or physical pain.) But the paradox is that when we make the effort to follow through without repeating ourselves or getting mad, discipline becomes easier. Our children learn that we mean what we say. Both younger children and teenagers often recognize that we have a threshold of resistance. They know exactly how long they can continue a behavior or keep up pressure before we get mad or give in. We can do ourselves and them a favor by keeping promises we have made and following guidelines we have set up.

If you find it inconvenient to carry out the consequences you set up, if your child pressures you until you give in, if your attempts at discipline often end up as argument, exploring the whole area of how to follow through can help you become a more competent disciplinarian.

Here are some suggestions for following through.

Give Up on Punishing

AMY (mother of two): "Maybe my ten-year-old just isn't mature enough to understand. I tell him again and again that I don't want him to do certain things and he seems to feel sorry when we talk about him doing them. He says he understands. But later he does it again. Sometimes I think he's just trying to get to me."

Repeatedly explaining or punishing (giving our child retribution for what he has done) are two of the most popular forms of discipline that frustrate both parents and children. No one likes to explain or hear explanations again and again. On the other hand, most parents don't enjoy punishing, but they see it as the only way their children will change their behavior. What many parents don't realize is that neither repeated explaining nor punishment has the desired effect.

Children can tune out explanations and punishments. We generally think of punishment—and the emotions or physical pain that go with it—as necessary to impress a child and make him regret what he has done. However, think back to your memories of being punished. You may recall that punishment often angered and humiliated you, or made you want revenge.

When we punish we usually do so in a way that demonstrates power over our child. That is part of the purpose of punishment—to remind him or her of who's in control. If children don't bow to power, we try to convince them by becoming more powerful. ("All right, if staying in your room doesn't make you want to say you're sorry, you can just go without TV tonight.")

The power struggles that result from attitudes like these can result in children looking for new ways to misbehave. One young mother says, "I remember when I decided that my parents were completely unfair and that I would defy them. They had grounded me for two weeks for a minor infraction. So I started sneaking out at night, crawling out of my window and meeting with my friends." Power-oriented discipline often breeds alienation and serious disruptions in relationships with children. But constant explaining or pleading with children won't insure that they meet our expectations either. The answer? We have to find ways of following through that help children learn from their mistakes.

One effective way to help children learn without making them angry or resentful is by using natural or logical consequences. Consequences arise from the situation, not from parental anger or a need for dominance. The issue of "who's in control" doesn't even have to be involved. But we do have to view discipline in new ways. We need to think about the possible consequences of a discipline situation so we won't have to fall back on punishment as the only solution.

Use Natural Consequences

Billy wouldn't eat supper, so his mother excused him. She warned him he wouldn't be able to eat after dinner. When he demanded a snack later, she had to follow through and say no.

Natural consequences arise from the situation. A parent may not have to intervene. If you don't eat, you get hungry. If you don't do your homework, you get marked down. If you don't get ready on time, you are late. If you don't wear a jacket, you get cold. If you forget your assignment, you won't be able to turn it in.

Many times adults protect children from the very consequences that would teach them, and then nag or punish them. For example, four-year-old Edie keeps playing with her food. Her father objects.

"If you don't eat, you won't get dessert."

"I don't care. I don't like it."

"You have to eat."

Nothing.

"OK, if you don't eat, you're going right to bed."

"I don't want to go to bed."

"Then you'd better eat."

In this example, Edie's father has turned himself into a power figure who has to win out over Edie's resistance to eating. He is determined to make her eat. But if she doesn't eat, she will be hungry later. And if she is not given a snack, she will learn that not eating her regular meals results in hunger. Her father is actually preventing this learning and is reinforcing her poor eating habits by paying so much attention to them. Using the original consequence of no dessert unless a certain amount is eaten is all that is needed.

Natural consequences can be presented in a positive way. Mary had a hard time eating her vegetables, so her family instituted a vegetable time *before* dinner was served. This was a little like a cocktail hour, with vegetables served in appetizing ways. The positive natural consequence was that dinner was served as soon as the vegetable course was eaten.

Use Logical Consequences

Jim warned his son not to leave his 10-speed bike on the lawn one more time or Jim would take it away. The next time his son left the bike out, Jim took it away for a week. A child can connect logical consequences with behavior. The parent's role should be to point out what the results of a particular behavior will be and then matter-of-factly carry out that plan.

"If you disturb other people at the table, you will have to leave it."

"If you don't put your clothes in the hamper, you won't have anything to wear."

"If you don't come to breakfast when it is served, you won't have anything to eat."

"If you jump on the couch, you will have to get off."

The goal of natural or logical consequences is the same: to shift responsibility for the way the child behaves from the parent to the child. If you hassle your child repeatedly about a behavior, then you are taking responsibility for it. The result is that he or she doesn't have to change.

"Do your homework." "Clean your fish tank." "Put away your bike." These are all statements that imply a parent's responsibility. Children can count on us to remind them until they grudgingly do whatever we are asking. However, if they don't do their homework, they might learn from a bad grade; if they don't clean the tank, they might learn from a dead fish; if they don't put the bike away, they might learn from a rusty or stolen bike.

Here are some of the ways parents prevent learning:

Many parents become ineffective by overprotecting their children. David's mother wants him to do well in school. When he tells her he has forgotten an assignment at school, she drives him back to get it out of his desk. She schedules David's time at home to do homework, and she helps him do all of it. Actually, she is working against her own goals. David knows that his mother will protect him from any negative consequences of his actions. He simply doesn't feel responsible for his own work.

Many parents cause bad feelings by inflicting unreasonable consequences.

"Do you think you can come home late? You're grounded for three weeks."

"You don't have your homework done? No TV for the whole weekend."

"If you hang out with those kids, you aren't going to use the phone anymore."

"You played in the puddle when I told you not to. You can't go outside the rest of the day."

"If you cause a fuss when I'm on the phone, you can't watch *Mr. Rogers* today."

These consequences are actually punishments.

The attitude behind each of them is the same: I want to get back at you; I want to make you sorry, to humiliate you for what you have done; I want to teach you who's boss. It's natural to be angry at our children sometimes, but our goal in discipline should be to *allow them to learn*. Parents often turn consequences into anger-causing punishments by using a negative tone or by not connecting the consequence with the behavior that caused it.

As an adult, Susie can recall the time in high school when she forgot about an important after-school meeting that kept her out past dinnertime. When she came home late, her parents grounded her for two weeks. She still remembers her anger.

Being grounded for two weeks is a lifetime to a child or an adolescent, and having to stay home for all that time breeds depression and a desire for revenge, not contrition. A *logical* consequence the first time your child comes home late might be making her call home a half hour before curfew the next time, or staying home from a date that weekend. These consequences are not overwhelming. They are connected with the original behavior, and cause the child to think about her actions so that she can avoid the consequences next time.

Parents may be too uncomfortable to allow children to live with the consequences of their actions. Diana had to go to bed early for three nights because she had refused to go to bed when the babysitter told her to. Diana fussed, but her parents followed through. It's hard to follow through when a child is upset. But we have to show that we mean what we say.

Using consequences often involves our ability to do nothing, and that can be more difficult than punishing. If your twelve-year-old doesn't call her grandmother, her grandmother will be upset with her. If your eleven-year-old doesn't feed his dog, his dog will go hungry. If the pattern continues, your son might not be able to keep his pet.

We don't have to invent hardships. We just need to think about what consequences are natural or logical in the situation and allow them to follow, despite the fact that it may make things temporarily uncomfortable or inconvenient.

Sometimes parents don't follow through because they are intimidated by a child's reactions. The story of Jason in the first chapter illustrates the problem so many of us have when our children's reactions upset us. We want to avoid disruptions in our relationships. When we are tired or under stress, it is especially difficult to follow through on some rule that seems unimportant for the moment. However, when we don't follow through, things can get worse. Children will take advantage and remind us that we allowed them to break the rule before, or they'll push us to find out what the rules really are.

Even if we are consistent, discipline can be upsetting to our children. No one likes to have his wishes thwarted, or to bear the consequences of a foolish action. When John arrives at school late because he refused to get ready on time, when Lauren isn't allowed to snack all day, they may grumble and test us to see if we will change our mind. However, they will also sense the fairness of the situation if it is logically connected to a problem we have discussed beforehand. When we follow through consistently, things become much easier over the long run.

Here are some natural and logical consequences:

- Throwing food out of a high chair—remove child from chair.
- Having a tantrum—walk away until child calms down.
- Older child borrowing something from you and losing it— have her replace it out of her own money.

- Losing a library book—have him use his allowance to replace it.
- Needing more money after allowance is gone—refer her to previous discussions on budgeting and help her set new goals.
- Having bad table manners—ask him to leave the table.
- Leaving a toy out in the rain after being asked to put it away—put toy in garage for two weeks.

Conclusion

Following through takes endurance. If they think there is a chance that we don't mean it, our children will argue, tell us we're unfair, cry, or otherwise pressure us. But we must develop our capacities for doing what we say. It's never too late to start, and the more we do it the easier it gets. Children—and even teenagers—are amazingly adaptable, and don't test us as much when they are used to the fact that we will follow through.

Whether you have always tried to follow through or are just beginning, do it matter-of-factly. If your actions aren't personal and punitive, your child won't feel compelled to resist you and you won't feel so vulnerable. When you make it a habit to follow through on promises, warnings, and consequences, your child will trust you—and feel more secure.

THE ABILITY TO WORK WITH OTHERS

ELLEN (mother of three): "When we were new parents, my husband and I had more arguments about discipline. We had different points of view and we didn't know how to work them out. But, over the years, we've learned to talk about discipline. The most important thing we learned to do is plan ahead. When something comes up, we talk about it alone and make up a strategy. That way we can have a united front."

We tend to think of discipline as something each of us does individually with a child. But discipline is almost always a collaborative process. Unless a child lives in isolation, he is raised with the guidance of many people, and he benefits when they can work together. These adults also need to work with children in setting up rules and determining consequences for behavior. If we can make children partners—give them choices, help them feel as if they can control their behavior—discipline will have more lasting effects and they will learn in the process.

Each adult brings a unique view of discipline to his experience with children, and the fact that we see things in different ways is no surprise. But we can benefit from diversity by pooling our joint learning, finding points of agreement, and working out strategies. People do this in other areas of life all the time, and discipline shouldn't be an exception.

If you and your spouse don't always see eye to eye on childrearing, if your child's teacher seems unfair, if you and your babysitter have different methods, concentrate on working *together* to help your child.

Here are some suggestions for working with others.

Accept Differences

Once we gain insights into our own style of parenting, we wonder why those around us don't automatically see things the way we now do. When our spouse or another parent maintains a different view, it can make our discipline problems seem harder to solve. But it shouldn't.

Our children don't have to suffer because we aren't carbon copies of one another. Teachers who work in the same school don't necessarily handle children the same way. They try to share information and agree on rules and the consequences for breaking them so that children experience consistency even amid a variety of personalities.

As our children grow, there will be many people involved in shaping their behavior, and they will benefit if those concerned guardians can work together. It helps if we see discipline as an open, mutually supportive process that includes others.

Those we need to work with include our spouses or housemates, our children, and anyone who shares in the care of our child (i.e., grandparents, aunts and uncles, teachers, child care workers, ex-spouses. It will also help us and our children if we include other parents with children the same age (to discuss issues), parent educators (to give us new ideas), and counselors (when we need to sort out a problem).

Work with a Spouse or Housemate

Bev and John tend to undermine each other's efforts. John believes in a tough, no-nonsense approach and thinks Bev is too lenient and overprotective. "When I misbehaved, my father would give me a whipping, and I'm a better man for it. I feel like Bev is ruining Steve by coddling him and never letting him learn what happens when he misbehaves."

Bev feels that John's methods are harsh. She was brought up by more lenient parents, and when John comes on strong with Steve, she jumps in to protect him. Until recently, Bev and John had never discussed their own childhood discipline experiences. When disciplining Steve caused heated arguments between them, they decided to talk. The first thing they discovered was that they each thought their own point of view was the "right" one and couldn't understand why the other's was so "distorted."

Talking helped them to be more empathic with one another. Neither of them had all the answers, they found, yet they both wanted the best for Steve. Looking back, John still felt pain because of the severe and arbitrary way his father treated him. John's father never seemed to think that John's feelings were important. Bev still had feelings of insecurity from her childhood, and wished her parents had provided clearer limits.

Realizing these differences did not bring Bev and John into instant accord, but it did make them aware that their divergent views were natural and that their challenge as parents was to try and collaborate. They've started to agree on appropriate behaviors for Steve; deciding what the consequences will be ahead of time helps them respond in similar ways. When they don't agree, that's OK too. They have found that differences in discipline only become disagreements when one feels that the other's approach is "wrong" and tries to "correct" it. If Steve does something to displease John or Bev, they can give each other the leeway to handle it as each sees fit. If one of them really objects, they can talk about it later—alone.

When spouses concentrate on working together, they often find that their approaches become more similar. Discipline becomes less of a hassle and more of a team effort. There is still work involved, but having sorted out differences makes it much easier.

Include Children in Problem-Solving

Start by thinking of discipline as something we do *with* children rather than *to* them. The first step in solving a problem should be to talk with our children about it and ask for their cooperation.

We might say to a four-year-old: "I don't want you to run in the house. How can we find a way to help you remember to walk when you're inside?"

To a seven-year-old: "It's hard to talk on the phone when it gets so noisy. What do you think we can do to keep things quieter?"

To a fifteen-year-old: "I worry about your walking to a friend's house after dark. What can we do to keep me from being anxious?"

Some schools have sessions when everyone in the class works together to develop rules. Then the rules are posted. Families can do that too.

Holding Family Discussions

Having regular meetings at which family members can bring up complaints and make decisions on issues such as family outings, schedules, and chores brings harmony to family life. Sometimes family discussions can be focused on a particular problem: Dad's tools were left out, or someone borrowed Susie's sweater and lost it. Having everyone's opinion keeps problems from becoming a battle between individuals. Getting the family to think about an issue usually reduces tensions and helps the members make commitments to try new behavior. Meetings can be run democratically, with everyone (down to the two-year-old) participating. Once a given solution is agreed upon, it can be evaluated at the next meeting.

The Hughes family had meetings to set up a rotation of chores. Jobs were written on pieces of paper and drawn out of a hat. They planned to swap jobs in a month. Meanwhile, during the next week, some problems arose. Rather than hassling about them with each other, they just set up another meeting. Having a joint discussion helped them work out their individual problems in a harmonious way.

Meet with Your Spouse or Ex-Spouse

Disagreements about discipline are a common source of conflict between parents. The problem can become more troublesome when parents divorce. A different style of discipline on the part of an ex-spouse can confuse and frustrate the other parent and the children. Divorce represents a loss, and parents often try to overcompensate for it. The result is sometimes chaos at a time when a child needs secure guidelines more than ever.

For example, David's ex-wife would often get involved in conflicts between him and their teenage daughter. It helped when he finally asked his former wife not to interfere. He pointed out that even her attempts to problem-solve with their daughter in a positive way undermined the girl's abilities to respond to him. She was used to depending on her mother and needed to form a new relationship with her father.

When both parents recognize the importance of talking about their children's needs and of remaining consistent in their goals, the children will not be confused in movement between households. Single parents can discuss their childrearing concerns with extended family, other parents, and friends.

Try these steps when you discuss your children's needs with those who share in their care:

Make a list. Itemize the things your children do that bother each of you. What are the priorities? Pick a problem from each list and agree to work on it in specific and consistent ways. What methods can you agree on? What are your goals? How can you support each other? Meet again to evaluate your efforts.

Talk about needs. Think of the kind of support each of you needs in order to be a better disciplinarian, and ask each other for help. Maybe Dad wants feedback on how he handles Tommy. Perhaps Mother doesn't like to make children do chores when she's tired. Adults can take over for each other. Compare your strengths and weaknesses on the discipline test and see where your strong and weak areas lie. How can you help each other?

Meet with Teachers and Other Professionals

Today, people who share in the care of a child can have radically different views. It is important to discuss discipline with a child's teacher or babysitter. Otherwise you may be working at cross-purposes.

Teachers and parents benefit from sharing information and talking about their goals and problems. Teachers should be aware when a student's parents are getting a divorce, or his mother is away on business, or his parents are being stricter with him.

Teachers, child care workers, and babysitters can also provide valuable information. It's important for parents to know that James defaced school property or that Karen's behavior is improving. Ask for information about your children's performance. Busy teachers or after-school workers may be reluctant to come to you with each problem. Let them know that you're interested, and make it easy for them to share their experience with you.

For example, Cathy was disturbed when she learned that her son Adam was bringing toys to school to sell. She immediately called the principal and was relieved to hear that the school staff felt the same way. They were in the process of setting up a rule to prohibit the sale or trading of toys, since children were tending to take advantage of each other in these situations. Checking in with the principal allowed her to handle the problem with Adam in an effective way before it got out of hand.

Meet with Other Parents

Find other mothers and fathers who have a child the same age as yours, and discuss parenting and specific discipline issues with them. Meet with parents in your child's class to discuss TV watching, allowances, and bedtimes, and try to come to a consensus about reasonable limits so that you can reinforce each other. One group of parents of sixth-graders met for several months to work on childrearing issues, adjusting many things to be more consistent as a result.

If your child has a serious behavioral problem, it can help to find other parents with the same difficulties. If your child is on probation, having problems at school, using drugs or alcohol, or acting out sexually, meeting with other parents can help you feel less isolated and helpless. Ask the school principal or talk to your pediatrician for references.

Work with a Counselor

There are certain behavioral problems that require the help of a trained professional. If you experience any of the following, consider talking with a counselor who specializes in child or family problems.

- If you consistently motivate your children by withdrawing your love or turning a cold shoulder to them when they've been "bad" . . .
- If you feel afraid that you might physically hurt your child in anger . . .
- If you feel concerned that you are disciplining in destructive ways and you don't know how to change . . .
- If your children seem out of control and/or engage in

destructive behavior—hurting themselves, others, or property . . .
- If arguing over discipline is hurting your marital relationship . . .
- If your child has started wetting the bed or soiling himself long after being trained and you don't know what to do but punish him . . .
- If you are afraid your spouse is disciplining in destructive ways or might physically hurt your child . . .

When we or our spouses haven't had models of good parenting, a counselor can help us develop a new example of how to handle things. We can replace our old images of parenting with new responses our counselor shows us.

Conclusion

Nothing can make parenting more difficult than feeling alone or isolated when a problem occurs, and nothing can help more than mutual support. Being a parent draws on our capacities to work with problems—each stage bringing fresh challenges for us and our child—so the ability to find shared resources and to garner support is important, if not crucial.

Hearing someone else talk about bedtime hassles with their two-year-old, or knowing that another parent's eight-year-old balks at doing chores, can make us feel a lot better. This is not because we wish problems on others; we simply need to know that our children aren't the only ones who cause their parents concern. When a counselor or another parent understands our feelings, we become more capable of facing our problems and dealing with them.

Cooperation and resourcefulness are skills that we need in every area of life, and they are especially important in parenting. The ability to live and work with others is the most valuable resource any person has.

Now that you have explored the five skills that make up authoritative discipline, let's turn to your expectations. Our ability to discipline depends on being clear about what we expect, and some expectations are more apt to make discipline go smoothly and encourage growth than others.

4

Expectations for Our Kids

Children who are self-confident tend to have parents who are nurturing, firm, and have high expectations for them. But what does having high expectations mean? Does it mean that you expect your child to have excellent behavior and manners all the time? We have all known parents who expect *too much* of their children, and the results are usually negative. When children try and then fail to meet their parents' demands, they are left with a sense of failure and incompetence.

Because there are no common standards for children today, parents are often surprised by how little or how much other parents ask of their children. What does expecting too much or too little mean in concrete terms? Some parents expect their children to be toilet-trained before they are two, others don't even approach the task until their children are closer to three. Some parents expect their children to contribute significantly to housework when they are eight or nine, while others are gratified if a child the same age remembers to brush her teeth.

AMERICAN PARENTS

Interestingly, American parents expect less of their children in general than most other parents in the world. One result is that American children tend to be less helpful and cooperative than their age-mates in other countries. Throughout most of the world, help with family chores is a given by the time children are of school age. It is also interesting that most eight- or nine-year-olds around the world help care for younger children. Research shows that this has two important results. First, when children are expected to help, they form responsible attitudes. Second, children who help care for younger siblings tend to develop helpful attitudes in general—attitudes that are less common in American children.

This generation of adults has been criticized for its apathy and its overconcern with self. Research seems to indicate that our children are following in the adults' footsteps. Many experts consider American children to be more ego-centered as they grow older than young people in other countries.

However, studies show that, in families where parents expect considerate behavior and react negatively to selfishness, children *are* more concerned with others. One way of judging expectations and their appropriateness is to examine their relationship to such qualities as consideration or helpfulness. Are those qualities emphasized in our homes, or is the focus more on everyday concerns?

It helps to emphasize consideration for others.

"How do you think your sister feels when you take her things without asking? What would you want to happen if she did that to you?"

Or:

"I would appreciate it if you could let me know ahead of time when you need a ride. It isn't considerate to let me know at the last minute. Next time this happens, I'll have to say no."

Age-Appropriate Expectations

One of the most confusing issues for modern parents is knowing what to expect of their children at various ages. How do you know if your toddler really understands that he's not supposed to climb on the couch, leave the backyard, or break those eggs? Can your six-year-old be expected to brush her teeth or make her bed without reminding? Does your eight-year-old understand that when he takes money secretly from your purse he is stealing? Is your teenager really aware of the responsibilities of driving a car? Setting up rules has to involve thinking through our expectations.

Look at Your Reactions

One of the ways to judge our expectations is to consider our own reactions. Do you feel your child should pay more attention when you're talking? Do you think your child could help without an argument, and then dismiss the thought because you don't have the time to train her? Are you frustrated because your child won't outgrow some babyish ploys for getting his own way? Pay attention to your instincts about these things. They offer valuable clues for judging discipline. From there we can check out our perceptions with other parents or with a teacher or counselor.

Expecting Too Much

When we are unwilling or too busy to help our children achieve expectations, then we may ask for such things in a way that makes the child feel incapable or inadequate. We can't *demand* that a five-year-old tie his own shoes or set the table. But many five-year-olds can do these things if their parents encourage, teach, and supervise them.

The same is true for different tasks at other ages. It's our interest and effort that helps children accomplish. When we're not consistent in our expectations or when we're not aware of the steps needed to be competent, children may feel that our demands are arbitrary or unfair. When we consistently try to make our children feel successful and show them how to be, we are likely to tailor our expectations to their capacities.

EXPECTING TOO LITTLE

One of the dangers of expecting too little of children is that it makes it harder to raise our standards for them at the next stage of development. It can be enormously difficult for a ten-year-old to stop talking back or whining, or speak to us respectfully if those negative behaviors have become ingrained. But even older children can change. Children are extremely adaptable and tend to adjust their behavior when they know an adult "means it." In fact, children become anxious when all of their negative behavior is accepted unconditionally. They feel more secure when they receive guidance on what is or is not appropriate.

CHECK WITH OTHERS

One way to think about expectations is to ask other parents what they expect from their children. You might select children whose behavior and manners seem especially appealing to you. Observe or talk to the parents about the rules of their home, and about the kind of behavior they feel is important. They may be able to suggest ways to work on problem areas that have worked well for them. Remember that changing your expectations of your child is not a process that can happen overnight and that you can't work on everything at once. It is more effective to change one or two expectations and help your children to meet them gradually.

EXPECTATIONS AND SELF-IMAGE

It's also important to realize that thinking about expectations for our children and trying to fit them to their capacities goes beyond trying to pick the chores they can do or deciding whether they're ready to do something on their own. Our overall expectations for our children—spoken or unspoken—teach them attitudes toward themselves and life.

Ronnie: "My mother always thought I was strong, so I looked at myself that way. I could endure things no matter how hard. I could be courageous. Later it seemed funny to think how her expectations conditioned me to see myself that way."

Abe: "Somehow nothing I ever did was good enough. It was a consistent feeling in everything my father said. If I got good grades, I still could have done better, or I could have gone out for some extracurricular activity. It got so I wouldn't tell my father things because it made me feel so vulnerable. It took away the feeling of success. As I grew older, it got very hard to make myself do things. It was hard to make the effort."

The expectations parents have teach children to look at themselves in certain ways. Perhaps, most importantly, expectations provide a basis for encouraging children to become problem-solvers or, conversely, to feel incapable of meeting life's challenges. The pattern of our expectations nurtures their abilities to accept responsibility—or increases their tendencies to run away from it.

What do your interactions communicate? Do we look on our child as responsible, or do we point out again and again what a failure he is at carrying out tasks? Do we expect our child to be considerate, and express our appreciation when she tries, or do we always complain about her selfishness? Do we expect our child to be able to do her homework and let her experience the consequences at school if she doesn't, or do we nag about it and say that she isn't a good student? We don't have to spell out what we think of our children. They can sense the kind of people we think they are.

In one study of adults who are considered to be tops in their fields—from music to science to athletics—a common theme emerged. Not all of the "geniuses" were considered extraordinary as children. What they did have in common were parents who nurtured and encouraged them to give their very best. A child carries our expectations away from a situation—how much we think he could do for himself, how capable we think he would be of learning a new skill, how we think he should treat others.

Our expectations should inspire our children toward positive behavior. That's why having high expectations doesn't mean we grab our children by the collar and say, "Look here, you'd better be responsible and kind—or else!" On the contrary, expectations should encourage a child's own desire to become those things and should make her realize she already possesses those capabilities and needs only to express them.

EXPECTATIONS AND DISCIPLINE PROBLEMS

If our expectations can inspire our children they can also at times be roadblocks to their growth. Many discipline problems are the result of confused, discouraging, or negative expectations. A father demands courage of his son, even when his son is afraid; the boy takes out his frustration on a sibling. A child continually forgets her lunch or her coat, and then demands that her mother bring them to school; her mother is convinced this irresponsibility can't be helped.

Children are also conditioned by the expectations we have for ourselves. If we tend to blame others for our problems rather than acting capable of solving them, our children will do the same. The opposite is also true. In the study of "extraordinary" people we referred to, subjects consistently reported that their parents provided strong examples of doing their best in their chosen activities.

Poor approaches to problem-solving, passed on from generation to generation, can also be responsible for discipline problems. In a profile of adolescents who had severe discipline problems, they tended to see themselves as victims with no power to affect their life situations. These unhappy young people tended to blame others for their problems, no matter what their experience.

They got bad grades because teachers didn't like them. They lost their job because the boss never told them what to do. They were expelled because the principal was unfair, and had it in for them. They were arrested because the cop wouldn't listen. And on and on.

Blaming others rather than trying to solve problems themselves is a pattern that can begin early in childhood if children observe it in their parents. When they are young, all children tend to blame others to some degree. When siblings fight, they typically point to each other as the one who started it. But children should gradually learn to take responsibility and admit when they're at fault. They need help to sort out what they are truly responsible for and what they aren't.

Dr. Denis Madden, a psychologist who has worked extensively with young people with severe discipline problems, comments: "So many of these young people have never been helped to feel control over anything in their lives. They have never learned to make choices, mostly because they were never offered choices. No one helped them to decide on options or made them feel they could make good decisions. They've usually observed others running away from problems and blaming them on other people from the time they were very young."

Helpful expectations encourage children to grapple with problems, and are based on the assumption that children can cope even when they make mistakes or the situation seems unfair. This takes sensitivity and effort on the part of the parent. As psychiatrist Scott Peck says: "Opportunities present themselves thousands of times while children are growing up, when parents can either confront them with their tendency to avoid or escape responsibility for their own actions or can reassure them that certain situations are not their fault. But to seize these opportunities, as I have said, requires of parents sensitivity to their children's needs and the willingness to take the time and make the often uncomfortable effort to meet these needs. And this in turn requires love and the willingness to assume appropriate responsibility for the enhancement of their children's growth."

Helpful expectations aren't always obvious. Most of us approach our children with the best intentions, but when we demand or force behavior, we meet with resistance and can be disappointed. Parents who insist on competence and count on their children's achievements to gain their own ego satisfaction may find that their children can't muster the motivation to achieve.

Developing helpful expectations is a learning process. It involves examining and reexamining our perceptions as our children grow and as we change. What we expect at one stage of our children's development will—and *should*—differ from what we expect at another. These changes will also affect the way our children behave as they get older.

When our thinking is confused or unrealistic, it can block our children's growth and our ability to give them what they really need. Of course, we can't know what our children need all the time, but paying attention to our expectations and trying to evaluate the roadblocks to their achievement increases our abilities to have helpful expectations. That is an ongoing process.

Let's look now specifically at different stages of development, and at what some helpful expectations and roadblocks to them might be.

Babies (newborn to one year)

What might helpful expectations for a baby be? Should we expect them not to cry, not to be upset when a stranger approaches, not to cling to us? Certainly not. Crying to communicate their needs, distinguishing caregivers from strangers, and forming "clinging" attachments to us are all positive aspects of a baby's development. When we respond to babies' needs, we nurture their ability to cope now and at the next stage of development.

Here are some general expectations that may be helpful for babies.

Predictability. It helps when we expect (not demand) that babies can live by a stable schedule. If we help them eat, sleep, play, and take outings at predictable times, they will develop a life rhythm. Having a rhythm will help baby now and in the future. Children feel more secure when their lives are tuned to regularity and they can predict what is going to happen.

For example, Nancy plans her outings with Dana at certain hours of the day. That way he gets a chance to nap at around the same time in the morning and afternoon and his rhythm isn't disrupted. In this fast-paced age, a schedule can be difficult to maintain. Parents have to work at keeping routines and to insure that their thinking is not a roadblock to providing predictability.

Roadblock: Bev wanted to be sensitive to her newborn's needs and wanted him to be spontaneous rather than a regimented person, so she was determined not to impose her schedule on him. She took him everywhere and tried to feed him when he was hungry, let him sleep when he was tired. But spontaneity exhausted Bev after a month. Her son had no routine she could predict. Bev's life revolved around meeting his needs twenty-four hours a day.

A friend finally helped Bev stay home more and balance her son's feeding and sleeping schedules. Soon he was eating at regular times and, because he was fuller at his feedings, he slept longer. Bev could predict how long she could rest or engage in her own activities.

Babies need predictability and we do, too. Predictability now provides for calm in the future, and gives us a storehouse of energy to cope with unexpected disruptions.

Solitude. Babies need to learn to play by themselves sometimes, to soothe themselves a little, and to tolerate being alone. We should expect them to learn this at times when they are not upset, so that they learn solitude in positive ways. For example, Kay programs times into every day when five-month-old Andrew can play alone. He gets so stimulated when his four-year-old brother is around that Kay wants to make sure he also gets quiet and time alone. She's learned to interpret his cries and always picks him up when he gets upset. But she finds that he can play alone longer now than he did even a month ago.

Roadblock: Alice couldn't stand to hear her baby fuss even for a minute. She was afraid Sara might feel lonely and rejected if no one was there when she woke up. So Alice arranged to have the baby near her while she did housework. Sara was a sensitive baby and seemed more so when no one was around. As a result, neither Alice nor Sara were ever alone. Alice didn't feel comfortable going into the yard or taking a shower when her daughter was awake. Whenever she tried to slip away, she found Sara crying. Finally, her style of mothering started causing problems with her husband. He didn't see why she had to jump whenever Sara cried. He felt it interfered with their relationship and their lives.

In truth, Alice isn't a neurotic mother. Sara *is* a fussy baby and has conditioned Alice to try and comfort her and make her happy all the time. But Alice's belief that Sara might feel lonely and rejected if left alone even for a moment is unrealistic. Sara does need to feel that her mother will respond when she is hungry or upset, but both also need solitude, if only for short periods of time. Otherwise, Sara may have difficulty learning to be alone and Alice will continue to feel constrained and pressured. If this roadblock continues, it could perpetuate a relationship in which Alice feels she has to give in or "do something" every time her daughter is upset. This is a common problem with first babies. It is likely, however, that as Sara grows out of her fussiness and crying, Alice should feel more comfortable with the idea of giving her some time alone.

Power. Babies need to feel that they can affect others. We should give them the sense that we will respond to their needs before they are overwhelmed by them. They should learn that when they cry or are upset, we will comfort them; when they smile, we will smile back; when they look at us, we will also look at them; when they talk, we will talk back.

Terry uses mealtimes, changing times, and dressing times as opportunities to have fun with her baby. She talks to Michael, tickles him, plays with him. When he does something new, they make a game out of repeating it. They play at other times, too, but Terry wants to make his routines fun.

Responding to babies gives them a natural sense of power, which infants need in order to thrive. Having power nurtures close relationships.

As soon as John comes home from work, six-month-old Michael gets very animated. Michael's eyes sparkle and his whole body leaps forward in enthusiasm. His father gets excited, too. John leans down, looks in his son's eyes, picks him up, and talks to him like a buddy. Each communicates to the other through glances, smiles, and expressive sounds. Michael is learning that he has the power to make people respond to him.

Roadblock: There are lots of traditional attitudes about "spoiling" babies that act as roadblocks to their real needs. David doesn't want his son to be spoiled. When the baby cries at night, he insists that his wife, Susan, refrain from going to him. When David comes home from work and hears his son fussing (as he often does before dinner), he objects to Susan holding the baby. "You're going to make a sissy out of him," David protests. "You can't just pick him up every time he fusses. He's going to learn to get what he wants through whimpering and crying. We've got to show him who's boss."

David's childrearing attitudes are those he himself grew up with. But they are based on old wives' tales and a view of children as little adults, rather than on an understanding of developmental learning in babies. Research shows that babies who have parents who respond to them consistently tend to be *less* fussy and clingy as they get older because they feel relatively secure. Babies who have been poorly responded to are more apt to fit the stereotype of the "spoiled" child as they get older. They are more likely to cling and be hard to comfort.

Research also shows that making a baby feel he can count on us to respond and that he has the power to affect us lead to positive behavior later in life. Babies who were observed to be more obedient at one year were not those who were given more commands or handled more strictly. On the contrary, they were babies whose parents were more attentive to their needs. Infants don't need to be held all the time. But feeling that their needs will be attended to aids them in feeling contented and in developing self-assurance. They are better prepared for the next stage of development, when they need to become more autonomous. Toddlers need to move away from their parents (and come running back to them), and they'll do that when their parents have proven that they'll be there when they are needed.

Giving a baby the power to affect his environment is the beginning of encouraging positive feelings of control and mastery over it.

Toddlers (ages one to two-and-a-half)

What should we expect of our toddler? Should she automatically comply with our wishes, be sensitive to our tiredness, respect our possessions and our need for order? Certainly not. Toddlers are propelled to move, to touch, to mouth, and generally to explore the world around them. They think of people as objects too. She'll pull your nose, climb over her best friend, and keep moving when we've lost the energy to stand. She isn't capable of empathy or of stifling her own wants in an effort to please us. She can't usually stop what she's doing simply because we tell her to. That's why a basic part of disciplining a toddler is learning to distract or even to move them bodily from one activity to another. "If you eat sand, you'll have to come out of the sandbox." "If you throw food, you must get down from your high chair." Toddlers have the ability to understand some of what we say long before they can articulate things. However, our actions speak louder and more effectively than our words, especially when we don't get angry or overreact. Toddlerhood is a crucial age for parenting because roadblocks in a parent's thinking can definitely set the pattern for problems with discipline later on.

Here are some examples of helpful expectations for toddlers.

Accessibility. Toddlers need access to their surroundings. They need to touch, climb on, crawl under, and generally manipulate things in their environment. They must not have access to everything, of course, but toddlers do learn from the stimulation of a rich, sensory world. If we accept the fact that exploration is an important learning activity for toddlers, we will be more apt to set up our homes in ways that are safe for them and don't require constant admonishments or attention.

Research shows that, under the impact of a baby who is

suddenly running all over the house, mothers tend to do one of two things: put their babies into playpens or other restricted play areas, or adjust the home environment to let them roam. Research findings indicate that doing the latter results in toddlers who know how to learn in more capable ways, even into the elementary years. Conversely, restricting babies to preserve our sanity can be a roadblock to their learning.

Joyce takes care of two toddlers during the day (her own and a neighbor's) to earn extra money. During the morning, these two active explorers follow her while she does housework. Sometimes they also go in the opposite direction from Joyce, or each of them takes off into a different corner of the house. But Joyce finds she only has to check on them from time to time because the house is babyproof. They still get into trouble and make messes, but Joyce feels that raising her two older children has helped her to be pretty relaxed around toddlers. These toddlers learn from Joyce, the environment, and each other. Problems arise if we see toddlers' naturally high activity levels as an obstacle in our lives.

Roadblock: Ann has just realized that being the mother of a toddler isn't as satisfying as nurturing her baby was. Her son Blake doesn't seem to need her anymore. On the contrary, some of his actions seem designed to provoke her: dumping his food on the floor, or taking all of his clothes out of the drawer when she has just cleaned his room. Blake is always on the go, never wants to cuddle, and won't give in when she asks him to do something. He just keeps doing his own thing and throws a tantrum when she opposes his wishes. Ann is thinking about going back to work full-time. She thinks she would feel less exhausted working eight hours a day than caring for Blake. Whether or not she goes back to work, Ann needs to work on her relationship with her son and adjust her expectations of him.

First, the idea that Blake is trying to "get to her" is not based on a realistic understanding of his thinking. Her son simply isn't capable of understanding or empathizing with her attitudes and emotions at his age. Blake is active because his own internal growth urges him to be that way, and he needs to explore and have an outlet for his energies. Secondly, Ann's way of stopping him from inappropriate behavior has led to power struggles that will escalate unless she finds a different approach. Ann needs to learn to distract her son and lead him toward positive activities. She also needs to set up the environment so that he doesn't have to be constantly interrupted in his explorations. When he throws a tantrum, she can put him in his room and leave him there until he calms down. Getting angry or spanking him will only increase his tendency to repeat negative actions in the future.

Both we and our children need to get used to one other at each stage of development. Evaluating and adjusting our expectations as our children change helps prevent discipline problems or solve those that already exist. This is especially true for toddlers, who often present as much challenge as adolescents. At both stages, avoiding power struggles is a crucial tactic for positive discipline.

Limits. Toddlers need clear limits. Although we expect less of a toddler than we do of an older child, we shouldn't let him behave in ways that would be considered out-of-bounds for an older child. Patterns of negative behavior are hard to unlearn later on.

The Stevenses have only a few rules for Josh, but those rules are consistent. For example: No hitting (his baby brother, the cat, his parents, or the children in the neighborhood—even the older ones who say it's OK). No running in the house. No playing with food or throwing it. Sometimes Josh has to be reminded of these rules, but at eighteen months he is starting to understand them. His parents don't get angry when he breaks the rules. They are matter-of-fact about enforcing them. If he hits, he has to stop playing or sit on a chair. If he runs, he has to go back and walk. If he plays with his food, he has to get out of his high chair. With simple rules like these, Josh's life is predictable. Toddlers get confused and often become more difficult when our expectations are not clear-cut.

Roadblock: At two, Adam already makes adults outside his family uncomfortable. He hits other children and when his parents tell him to stop he hits them too and says "I hate you." His parents see his behavior as a stage, part of being a "terrible two-year-old." At other times he's so charming and loving that they've learned to tolerate his negative behavior. They tell Adam that he shouldn't hit his friends, but they allow him to continue playing when he does. In general, they ignore his verbal outbursts because they've heard that when you ignore negative behavior it is more likely to go away.

Unfortunately, this isn't the whole truth. Josh needs to experience some negative consequences when he disturbs others. When there are consequences children care about, they are motivated to learn more positive ways of interacting. Adam might be removed from play with others when he hits, or be sent to his room when he screams "I hate you." Ignoring his tantrums can be appropriate, too.

Expecting positive social behavior from toddlers—even if they can't always meet our expectations—is part of teaching them. Relying on them to give up negative behavior on their own isn't usually realistic. It helps when we actively work toward positive behavior, but we shouldn't expect negativity to disappear overnight. If Adam's family picked one or two behaviors to work on (i.e., hitting and shouting) and praised him when he settled conflicts in more positive ways, they might be surprised that his behavior could gradually be improved.

Decision-Making. We have said that babies need to experience the power to make others respond. Toddlers need positive power, too. We can aid them in wanting to please and in becoming more independent by encouraging them to make some decisions for themselves. We have a negative stereotype of toddlers: They have a reputation for always saying no. But refusing others is just a way of asserting independence. When we understand that and give toddlers well-thought-out choices, it helps their development.

Robin's babysitter, Bertha, is a master at getting toddlers to cooperate. She's been doing it for almost a decade, and considers herself a toddler expert. She asks Robin if he would like to put his toy down now and have juice, or if he would like to put it down in a few minutes. If he chooses to wait but then doesn't comply when she returns, Bertha gently helps him put it down and then distracts him by taking him to the table. She then asks him what kind of juice he wants—orange or apple—and he forgets to cry over his toy. These simple choices go on throughout the day. As a result, Robin and his babysitter rarely have power struggles. She is always one step ahead of him and he doesn't even know he's being managed. Problems arise when we feel we have to meet a toddler head-on.

Roadblock: Mike is home with Susie more than his wife is. Greta works and he goes to school, so he calls himself a househusband. But, liberated parent that Mike is, he is beginning to be more and more frustrated by his daughter's willfulness. He feels that Susie should mind when he tells her to, whether the issue is putting away her toys or eating her lunch. When Susie blandly refuses or walks away, Mike sees red. But not even spanking helps. Susie just ends up crying and the issue is lost. To make matters worse, Greta says he's too tough on Susie and takes Susie's side when all three of them are at home. Mike is ready to throw in the towel.

Mike could ease his frustrations and have a more pleasant relationship with his daughter if he didn't see discipline as a need to control her. Feeling that he must exercise power over her and command obedience is a roadblock that makes their life together an endless power struggle. If Mike showed Susie that he would let her make some choices, and if he tried to motivate her toward positive behavior, she would be better behaved. A parent who is locked into power struggles with a child will almost always lose. And, if he doesn't lose that particular skirmish, he *will* lose out in their overall relationship. Children get angry in power struggles and become harder to handle. Well-behaved children want to please their parents; the positive relationship they share makes children *want* to comply with their parents' wishes.

Taking care of a toddler all day is challenging. But Mike could make things easier for himself and for Susie. Instead of demanding that she eat whatever he puts in front of her, he could ask if she wants soup or a sandwich. At this age choices must be simple, but offering them motivates children toward the desired activity. The goal of discipline is to motivate, not to control. Power struggles always produce an energy drain, so it's important to remember that the point of these interactions is not to "win out" against a child.

Preschoolers (ages two-and-a-half to five)

What should we expect of our preschooler? Should she be able to empathize with others? Her friends? Her parents? Should she be able to understand our explanations, and never repeat an offensive behavior? Yes and no. If we expect our preschoolers to *try* to understand other people's feelings and points of view, they will become more empathic over time—not overnight. If we explain why we have certain rules, our preschoolers will learn to reason and gradually can adapt to our expectations. If we teach our children to clean up after playing or working on a project, eventually they will learn to maintain their environment.

Realistically, preschoolers aren't really capable of consistent empathy, of understanding our thinking, or of cleaning a room by themselves. But when we encourage them toward these behaviors—step by step—they can achieve them in the next stage of development. Parents who assume that preschoolers understand other people's feelings but are deliberately hurting them, or that preschoolers don't need explanations or aren't capable of cleaning up, can have school-age children who are less mature than their peers. We need to encourage the behaviors we want to see in their next stage of growth.

Here are some helpful expectations for preschoolers.

Reasoning. The newly developed verbal abilities of preschoolers make them better candidates for explanations than their younger brothers and sisters. Preschoolers can shock us with their articulateness. However, large vocabularies and fluency often exceed their understanding. Explanations need to be short and emphasize the results of negative actions: calling names hurts other people's feelings and makes them mad; jumping on the couch breaks it. Once we've explained the reason for our displeasure, we can communicate the consequence if bad behavior continues. "If you call names, you will have to sit away from your friends for a while." "If you jump on the couch again, you'll have to go to your room."

Sadie likes to get her children to think. When they were driving along and Donnie threw some paper out the window, she asked him a simple question: "What would happen if everyone did that?" Donnie tried to come up with an answer. "There would be a mountain of paper," he said. This provoked a discussion about littering that engaged them all the way home. Sadie favors reasoning because she wants her children to think through their actions so they can act sensibly when she isn't around. The reasoning process that Donnie engages in with his mother now will help him make good decisions in the future. When we don't tell preschoolers the reasons behind rules, they won't learn to reason for themselves.

Roadblock: Annie likes to think of herself as being strict. She has four children (ages one through six), and if she doesn't run a tight ship, she feels things would fall apart. She is the main disciplinarian in her family. Her husband, Jim, is much more easygoing with the kids and leaves it to her to make them behave. Annie prides herself on having to threaten her preschoolers only once with losing dessert or going to bed without dinner to get them to shape up. It doesn't take a lot of explaining or repeating, and Annie is proud that her children always behave. Annie is a strong and consistent disciplinarian, but her emphasis on threats and commands without explanations is a roadblock in her thinking.

Preschoolers need to know why they should or shouldn't behave in specific ways. When people reason with a child, she learns to reason with herself. She can learn to ask herself some of the same questions adults ask her even when they're not around. If I threw this, would it break? Make a mess? Hurt someone? When parents use power techniques, it's difficult for children to learn to reason independently and make good decisions as they grow older. When children learn to reason in their preschool years and have firm limits set for them, they're apt to withstand pressure from others better and to think for themselves about what is right and wrong.

Limits. Although learning the reasons for rules—and even helping to develop the rules themselves—is important for preschoolers, explanations are not enough. To motivate real change, parents must allow preschoolers to experience natural or logical consequences. If he disturbs people at the dinner table, he needs to eat elsewhere. If she doesn't pick up her blocks from the living room floor, she won't be able to build with them outside her room next time.

Daniel knew the rules at home and quoted them to his friends sometimes when they came over. If there was no rule and he didn't think something was quite right, he made up his own. His most famous rule was "No jumping on guitars." His family still loves to tell that story and laugh at Daniel's resourcefulness in making a rule so quickly. But they also feel that having rules and consequences helped him to learn the principle of getting others to behave more positively— even someone who's about to jump on a guitar. If a child doesn't learn consistent rules, he will test for limits.

Roadblock: Three-year-old Daria is much more rambunctious than her older sister, who is six years old. It's hard to know how to handle her. She's also very charming, and when she does something wrong, she protests that she won't do it again. Then she forgets her promise and colors on the wall or pours water on the floor. Her parents lecture her, but with little effect. Daria continues to do what she wants.

Daria needs to experience limits, not just hear about them. Some children are very active and it's hard to monitor them. But if Daria's parents are willing to follow through and apply simple consequences now, their job will be easier later on. If Daria writes on the wall, her crayons should be taken away for a significant period of time. If she pours water on the floor, she should have to wipe it up. There is no "right" consequence for an inappropriate behavior. Parents have to think about what will affect their children and aid their learning. The principle here is to relate the consequence to the "crime," so that the child can learn from each situation.

Delayed Gratification. Although they may try very hard to convince us otherwise, preschoolers *don't* have to get what they want when they want it. Learning to wait a bit and to think of other people's needs in addition to one's own are part of becoming a considerate person. Few parents expect preschoolers to sit in one position or be silent for long periods of time, but if they can be taught to wait for a little while, the process yields positive results.

At Sally's preschool, the children wait to eat their snacks until everyone is served. They say a blessing before they start. Sometimes it's hard not to drink her juice or eat her crackers right away, but Sally feels that this bit of self-control is important. When children learn to pressure adults to get what they want immediately, the inability to delay gratification can become a habit.

Roadblock: When Laura picks up Amy from day care at 5:00, she is often greeted with protests and tears. "I wasn't ready to leave! Why did you come so early?" Amy shouts. Amy then insists that Laura sit down while she finishes what she was doing. When they get into the car, Amy says that she's starving and can't wait until they get home for dinner. She begs Laura to stop at Quick Stop for a snack; if Laura won't, Amy cries because she is "so hungry." Laura wants to begin her evening with Amy in a pleasant way, so she often gives in, but she's frustrated with Amy's self-centeredness. Waiting at the day care center and then shopping at the store delays dinner. By the time the dishes are cleaned up, it's bedtime. This leaves no time for play. Laura feels guilty about leaving Amy in day care all day and fears that may be why she's so overwrought when Laura picks her up.

Laura's feeling that she has to indulge Amy because she's in day care is a roadblock for many parents. Amy needs to learn that throwing a tantrum, crying, or demanding are inappropriate. Whether or not Laura gives in should depend on the situation, not just on Amy's strong responses. Laura shouldn't have to wait for her daughter to play at the end of the day. Expecting her to come right away most of the time is not unreasonable. Laura could also pack a nutritious snack for Amy to eat on the way home. That way she could comfortably say no to stopping at the store. Preschoolers benefit from learning that their needs have to fit other people's. Otherwise, they will make demanding things a habit.

Consideration. Although it's difficult for a preschooler to put himself in someone else's shoes, he can be taught consideration. If we point out other people's feelings, act considerately ourselves, and expect him to be kind and respectful, he will develop caring behavior. Kim usually talks to Tommy before his grandmother comes to visit. She explains that noise makes Grandma nervous, so they talk about ways he can play quietly. They also think of things that would make Grandma happy: showing her some of his artwork or singing one of his school songs. Kim finds that this kind of preparation helps visits to run smoothly, and Tommy feels he was a big help.

We want to encourage children to feel that they are helpful and considerate. We can do that by motivating them to act in ways that please others. If we don't emphasize considering others, children grow up with self-centered attitudes.

Roadblock: Aaron is an extremely active and aggressive four-year-old. He doesn't just walk into a room; he erupts into it. Aaron's parents could spend all their time trying to discipline him. But they have decided that they don't want to make Aaron feel badly about himself, so they try to accept his behavior. The trouble is, Aaron's actions affect others negatively. He takes things out of his twelve-year-old sister's room and breaks or loses them. He bugs her when she has friends over, or when they're riding in the car. When they visit friends, he gets into fights with other children and takes their things without asking. Aaron's mother may not be aware of it, but her nonintervention asks others to accommodate themselves to Aaron rather than teaching him to be considerate.

Deciding that his behavior is simply part of a stage he will outgrow is a roadblock. Aaron's parents don't have to be "on his case" all the time, but they do need to give him guidelines for interacting with others. He shouldn't be allowed to go into his sister's room or touch her things uninvited. He has to learn that hitting her or anyone else is completely unacceptable. He'll learn by having those things explained in terms of how the other person feels and by experiencing the consequences of his actions.

If he destroys something of his sister's, he should have to pay for it out of his allowance or otherwise make amends. If he hits, he should be removed from the immediate situation and be made to sit apart for a while. Aaron may be in an active and erratic stage of development, but now is the time to help him learn to control his impulses. His parents can communicate that they accept him and his activity level while they also point out what kind of behavior they expect.

Helpfulness. We should provide preschoolers with opportunities to help and train them to contribute in competent ways. If we expect and appreciate their help, they will see themselves as helpful people. Starting with self-help (getting dressed, making their bed, brushing their teeth, picking up toys), preschoolers can gain independence and make our schedules easier. Children of this age can also learn the value and satisfaction of reaching out to and helping others in a variety of ways: making a card for Grandpa, helping a younger sibling get dressed, watering a plant, answering the phone in a polite way. When helping is valued, we can build children's motivations to assist us. We usually connect helping with doing chores, but children need to see that helping can occur in many different ways.

Four-year-old Angelina has important jobs. She puts the silverware on the table for breakfast and dinner. She makes her bed every day, and puts her clothes into the drawer. But her favorite task is watering the plants. She knows the plants love to "drink," and feels proud that she is the one to quench their thirst.

Roadblock: It takes time and consistency to train children to be helpful. When we don't take the time, getting our children to cooperate can become an ongoing hassle. Sally hasn't got time to help Evan make his bed in the morning, even though she wants him to learn. Her schedule is just too rushed, and mornings are the worst time of all. She has talked to Evan about helping, and they agreed that he would put his cereal bowl on the table for breakfast and help clear up after dinner. But he usually wants to watch TV, and Sally is too tired to coax him to follow through with their agreement, so she does his jobs. Lately Evan hasn't been eager to help; when he does feel like helping, he wants to do a job he isn't ready for, such as washing the car.

The roadblock here is that Sally doesn't make Evan's help in small ways a priority. Preschoolers are usually eager helpers, and we need to encourage them to follow through. If we turn them down or don't teach them real skills, their enthusiasm wanes. Sally needs to take time to help Evan complete his responsibilities.

School-age Children (ages six to twelve)

What should we expect from a school-age child? Should he be more responsible, organized, and considerate than his preschool brother? Should he follow through on chores, homework, or practicing a musical instrument? Should he be motivated to achieve academically? Not automatically. These are the years when we can *gradually* encourage our children toward these qualities; there's still a lot of difference between a six- and a twelve-year-old. During these years, our children's image of themselves becomes more crystallized and their experiences in the world and at home will condition them to feel like successes or failures. They are more concerned with what other people think and feel about them, so we need to be sensitive to how they view themselves.

Responsibility. Children learn responsibility through having responsibilities. That may seem like an obvious statement but it isn't as simple as it sounds. Research shows that children who are expected to do chores, care for younger children, and take care of plants and/or animals actually develop more responsible attitudes. No amount of lecturing about responsibility can replace the experience of carrying out tasks. As mentioned earlier, American children tend to have fewer responsibilities than their peers around the world, and it is not surprising that they have less cooperative attitudes. With more mothers working, the actual supervising and training of children becomes more difficult. Learning new tasks in order to contribute to the family or help someone else takes time. But training children step by step is worth it because then they can gain self-confidence, and everyone will benefit from the skills they've learned.

Seven-year-old Mari likes to shine things. She will happily shine silver. She shines the chrome on the stove and on the refrigerator, and sometimes she does windows. She is considered the house expert on shining.

Roadblock: Vicki was surprised when her mother called about Lila. Both grandmother and granddaughter had looked forward to a time together during the summer. But Vicki's mother was irritated on the phone, "Lila doesn't pick up after herself. She leaves her clothes around, and makes snacks and leaves the plates for me to wash. When I ask her to set the table, she says she'll be there in a minute but it takes so long I do it myself. I could excuse her when she was little, but I'm surprised, Vicki. A ten-year-old should know enough to be responsible and help. You did at that age and I'm not asking her much. But she doesn't do anything at all."

That made Vicki think about her expectations for Lila. It was true getting Lila to help seemed more trouble than it was worth, but Vicki thought all kids were that way. Because we don't have standards for what children should be able to do, it's easy to get confused about responsibility. But feeling that getting a child to help is too much trouble is a common roadblock that can add to our problems. If Lila doesn't get in the habit of helping now, she's going to be much harder to handle as a teenager. Vicki needs to have concrete expectations for Lila every day and, if Lila doesn't fulfill them, there should be a consequence. It's perfectly fair to ask her not to play or watch TV until her jobs are done. On the other hand, she should be praised and receive incentives when she makes positive efforts. Children of Lila's age can soon become helpful people, but not without our encouragement and consistent efforts.

Perseverance. The school-age years are what the renowned psychologist Erik Erikson called the "age of industry." Children learn new skills, but more importantly they learn to apply themselves—they learn, in effect, to work. They form work habits and attitudes toward learning. Maybe they become people who try hard, or maybe they'll learn to give up after the first go-round. Parental attitudes toward these processes are vital. Some parents push children to excel and are disappointed by any failure. Some are too busy to be aware of the challenges their children are facing, and don't help them to cope. But if parents concentrate on encouraging children and praising them for making an effort at their tasks (as opposed to winning or succeeding), children can learn the invaluable quality of perseverance.

Once children enter school there is the danger that parents will become overinvolved with their children's achievements. Did you get that homework done? What grade did you get? Some parents exert so much pressure that their children develop psychosomatic illnesses or become depressed. Sometimes parents even do the work for their children. If we want children to learn perseverance, we have to walk a thin line between encouraging them and letting them experience the consequences of their efforts (or lack of effort). That's how they can become motivated to try, whatever the result.

As it turned out, Michael's soccer team was on a losing streak. His father went to every game, but never dwelt on whether the team won or lost. He always showed his appreciation for Michael's enthusiasm and efforts. Afterward, the two of them would go out together, and whatever the score, they always celebrated a game well played.

Roadblock: Jamie doesn't want his father to help with homework, but doesn't want to hurt his feelings by telling him this. His father's exasperation when Jamie makes a mistake in math or spelling is discouraging. He makes Jamie go over things again and again. Jamie doesn't know how to say, "But this is my work, Dad. Can't I figure it out for myself?"

Actually, his father's overinvolvement saps Jamie's motivation to learn and be responsible. Feeling that he has to make sure Jamie does his homework well, he is in fact hindering his son's academic success. Jamie needs to regard his schoolwork as his own, even if it means learning from his failures. The appropriate way to handle schoolwork would be to let Jamie ask for help only when he felt it was needed. His father may have different ideas or standards than Jamie's teacher, and Jamie shouldn't have to answer to two authorities. If his father is willing to let go of his own ego involvement in Jamie's success or failure, Jamie will have the opportunity to learn good work habits and to get in touch with his own motivation to persevere.

Limits. School-age children need to participate in discussions concerning the making of rules. Even in the early grades, their thinking develops and they can learn to put themselves in someone else's shoes. They are learning the reasons behind rules and why people break them. They benefit from reasoning and are more apt to be committed to positive behavior when their parents respect them rather than arbitrarily "laying down the law."

As children of this age extend themselves out into the world, they need to feel that limits are still secure but that new privileges can be earned. As they prove their ability to be responsible and do what they promise to do, children can be allowed to ride their bikes farther, go new places, and do new things. But the reverse is also true: When mutually agreed upon guidelines are abused, corresponding privileges need to be removed—at least temporarily. The child who doesn't come back when he said he would may not be able to visit his friend next time. It is this negotiating and renegotiating—with fairness and consistency—that makes setting limits successful. When parents aren't fair or consistent, things can get out of control.

One day Evelyn came home from work and found her twelve-year-old daughter entertaining some neighborhood boys. She was surprised because she had set up a rule with Dawn that people weren't to come into the house when she wasn't there. But Dawn had felt awkward when the boys came to the door. The boys had never done this before, and she was too shy to say they couldn't visit. Evelyn understood her daughter's predicament and they both agreed it wouldn't happen again. But she did make it clear that if Dawn couldn't abide by the rules of staying alone she would have to have a sitter for a while. She also suggested that if the same thing happened again Dawn could say something like "Let's sit out on the steps" or "I can get together around 5:00 when my mom gets home." Having some responses in mind to this potentially awkward situation helped Dawn feel more secure.

Evelyn and Dawn have a relationship that promotes mutual problem-solving and the establishment of fair rules. Dawn feels that her mother doesn't always jump to blame her; Evelyn tries to understand when things go wrong so they can work out situations together. This is a good basis for discipline in the adolescent years to come. Dawn enjoys her mother but respects her authority.

Roadblock: Lana and her eleven-year-old, Ann, have an intense relationship. They live alone and consider themselves more like sisters than mother and daughter. Lana prides herself on their closeness and on the fact that she doesn't play the role of disciplinarian with her daughter. There are few rules in the house because Lana and Ann rarely disagree. In fact, Lana has rarely had to take a stand with her daughter. But lately Ann has been pushing certain issues that Lana feels uncomfortable with, such as going to R-rated movies with her friends or wearing makeup. Lana usually gives in because she doesn't want to play the "heavy," yet she still feels uncomfortable. She doesn't want to disrupt their relationship by being the traditional kind of disciplinarian, but she doesn't want Ann to become a rebellious adolescent either.

Many adolescent discipline problems actually begin years before children become teenagers. The patterns often become intolerable as children get older. When parent and child are close, it can be uncomfortable to play the role of disciplinarian—especially if a single parent is involved. But this is what Ann needs. She needs a mother who can set limits and stick by them, as well as a mother who can be a friend. Sometimes it seems that taking the risk to impose discipline will lose us our children's affection. But we must take that risk, even when they get mad or say we're unfair. If we think ahead and plan out rules together we will be more likely to discipline calmly and fairly.

When we are fair, we don't have to worry about our children trying to manipulate us. Lana's mother may think it's late in the game to start treating her daughter in new ways, but that isn't true. Young children and adolescents too are adaptable, and are often relieved when we set firm limits—although we can't expect them to show it. As mentioned earlier, unclear or inconsistent rules (permissiveness) can cause them to have lower self-esteem.

Sometimes it's hard to take a stand if we are parenting in isolation. But even when children complain that "Everyone else is allowed!" we don't have to be afraid to say no. It can help Lana if she talks with other parents about the kinds of limits they set, so she will feel more secure in her own expectations. But it is also fine for her to have different views; children have to learn to live with the fact that other people sometimes do things that they can't. Lana can begin to discipline in a new way by thinking about guidelines she wants to set up at home, explaining them to Ann ahead of time, sticking to them, and following through on the consequences if they are not adhered to.

Manners. The subject of manners sometimes becomes an issue with school-age children. We expect them to say "please" and "thank you," not to interrupt conversations, and in general to act more civilly than their younger brothers and sisters. School-age children actually have more arenas in which to demonstrate manners: the classroom, the sports team, the after-school group, etc. But manners are only the external trappings of our real expectations for our children, which are that people should treat each other with kindness and consideration.

The word psychologists use for these traits is pro-social. Pro-social qualities are those that reflect a concern for others. Some psychologists are so concerned with the decline of these qualities in our culture in recent generations that they have made extensive studies on how they develop. In fact, the Child Development Project, operating in San Ramon, California, has been given a five-year grant by the Hewlett Foundation to implement a program that will develop pro-social qualities in children: helpfulness, consideration, cooperation, kindness, and honesty.

Jimmy has a special project in fifth grade this year. He tutors a third-grader in reading. The two have formed a close relationship and Jimmy looks forward to their times together twice a week. Tutoring has given Jimmy self-confidence and made him more sympathetic to other children's needs. When he sees his little friend at the playground now he stops and talks to him rather than just going off with his older friends or making fun of the younger children when they get in the way. Jimmy is learning pro-social attitudes through this innovative project.

During the school years a child's thinking changes. He develops a greater capacity for understanding the feelings and misfortunes of others than he had as a preschooler. Gradually being able to put himself in other people's shoes can make him more receptive to new and positive ways of interacting. However, research shows that pro-social traits are not developed automatically—they are learned. If parents and teachers stress a concern for others in their daily interactions, children are more likely to learn kindness and consideration.

Roadblock: Dick and Ivy fight a lot about Andrew's manners. Dick feels their son should have better table manners and that if he can't eat properly, he should be asked to leave the table. Ivy feels he will learn manners naturally, through observation, and objects to having conflict at the table. In the meantime, eight-year-old Andrew continues to eat quickly and sloppily so he can get back to watching TV.

Ivy's feeling that manners develop naturally is a roadblock in thinking that is common to many parents. But this misapprehension isn't limited to the area of manners: Parents also feel that children learn to share or to cooperate naturally. But most positive ways of interacting with others are *learned*. If we expect children to be considerate and to act positively, then we must help them develop the skills to do so in each situation. It doesn't help to say "You better have good manners!" or "Can't you get along?" We need to help children develop specific skills and ways of handling situations. Positive reinforcement is best: "Please stand up when you are introduced to our guests"; "Let's try to get along by not touching each other while we are driving in the car."

If Dick and Ivy can agree that they want Andrew to behave in ways that make other people happy and to be concerned about others' feelings, manners needn't become an issue between them. They can teach him those underlying principles so many ways. They can say things like "It makes people happy when we eat neatly" or "I need to ask you to stop kicking the table leg or fighting with your sister." Emphasizing the reasons behind manners helps children to understand our values. They don't automatically know that we are concerned about others or that we try to make them happy. Research on role modeling shows that hearing the reasons why *we* do things in certain ways improves the chances that children will imitate our behavior. A parent might say, "I'm setting the table in a special way because I want to make our guests happy"; or "I'm going to call Grandma because I think she's probably feeling lonely and I want to cheer her up." The point is to emphasize the positive motivation behind our manners.

Organization. As school-age children get older, more and more of their tasks require organizational skills, such as keeping up with homework, keeping their school desk neat, writing down an assignment, and keeping games and sports equipment in order for easy access. It helps children if we expect them to organize their world, but expecting organization is futile unless we teach them skills. Some of the most troublesome discipline problems today result from conflicts over disorder. On the surface it looks as if parents want and demand order but that children, perhaps because of some developmental kink, revel in disorder. This isn't true. Parents may not understand that when organization is a problem children haven't been taught the skills they need to create order. If organization is broken down and learned in parts, working with children on acquiring skills can be satisfying rather than overwhelming.

Joy learned a basic lesson. When she would simply say, "Steven, go clean your room," she would find him dawdling an hour later, surrounded by the same mess, going through his baseball cards. He didn't know where to start. But if she broke down the job into specific steps, her son could clean his room in a way that worked for both of them. She would write out a list: "Put all dirty clothes in the basket. Fold and put away all clean clothes. Take everything off bed and sort it. Put each item where it belongs . . ." Joy also worked along with her son because she knew that doing housework by yourself isn't as much fun. When children don't learn organizational skills, many areas of life can become confused.

Roadblock: Dolly gets frustrated with her homework and even throws a tantrum when she can't understand it. She sits on her bed with all her books and papers surrounding her and often misplaces the pages she has already done. Then she gets frantic and yells for help. Her mother begs her to work at her desk but Dolly refuses. She says it isn't comfortable because she likes to stretch out. Dolly's mother says Dolly will have to learn the hard way.

We can't force children to work at a desk, but we can give them skills to organize their work. The idea that Dolly will have to learn on her own is a roadblock in her mother's thinking because organizational skills must be learned. Many adults live in chaos because they never learned them. Dolly needs to separate out her papers according to subject matter, and divide finished assignments from those still to be done. Much of organization is sorting and dividing for easy access. These processes can be aided with the right equipment. Dolly could use plastic bins for different categories of papers, and keep those bins next to or under her bed. She could use file folders or cardboard boxes—whatever worked for her. But half of being able to understand her homework hinges on being able to organize it.

Adolescents (ages thirteen to nineteen)

What should we expect from adolescents? Should we ask them to think in adult ways? To be capable of understanding our logic? To be responsible? To follow through on what they say? Not automatically. It is true that adolescents *are* capable of a different kind of thinking than their younger brothers and sisters. If their powers to think have been nourished through reasoning and experience, they are often capable of true logic. That means they aren't restricted to their own egocentric point of view. They can examine different viewpoints and choose among them. On good days they can even put themselves in someone else's shoes—but not necessarily ours.

With these budding abilities comes a new challenge. Not only can they see the world in more flexible ways, but suddenly they are aware—even hyperaware—of how the world sees them.

Their perceptions may not be accurate, however. They may be flavored by anxiety about acceptance and by an adolescent self-absorption that magnifies every aspect of their being. "I can't go out on the street with this pimple. Everyone will be looking at it." "I can't wear that dress. Everyone would laugh at me." Teenagers may make life difficult for us with their intense reactions, but these feelings are a necessary and normal part of building an adult identity, even though they often limit the adolescent's new abilities to think logically. It's hard to be objective when you're emotionally overwrought.

Discipline poses new challenges at this age because emotions are so intense, desires are so intense, pressures are so intense. And it's hard to predict, when we talk to a teenager, which part of her will be responding—a sophisticated woman of the world or a little girl who wants to sit in our lap and be cuddled. If we can accept these fluctuations and their intensity, and provide security through firm and loving expectations, raising a teenager can be fun.

Positive Self-Image. Discipline is a crucial part of supporting an adolescent's positive self-image. In adolescence especially, self-esteem is torn down or built up in discipline situations. Parents who praise young people for their efforts, express appreciation for their help, and think of their children as basically good people can encourage them to think well of themselves. Teenagers need us to respect their new maturity and ability to think for themselves. Negotiating about rules, having fair consequences, and listening before judging are practices that help us preserve our relationships with our children—and leave our adolescent feeling good about himself.

When parents try to motivate teenagers through criticism ("You're just plain lazy," "I can't trust you to be responsible!" "All you care about is yourself"), young people are apt to live out these assessments. This is true at every age, but especially for teenagers, who are in a heightened process of deciding who they are. Yet parents who traditionally have used verbal putdowns in the hope of motivating their children can still change this habit when their children are teenagers. It's never too late to form a new basis for a relationship.

When James and Edie were first married, Daniel (James's fifteen-year-old son by a previous marriage) continued his typical response to life—anger and sarcasm. But Edie didn't mind.

She ignored his hostile retorts when she asked him to do things. Once, when he screamed, "You're not my mother," she replied warmly, "Of course I'm not. This has nothing to do with your mother. I'm just the other adult living with you, and I need help right now." Several months later, when Daniel needed something, he asked jokingly, "Where's the other adult in my life? I need help." Because Edie consistently acted as if he were the loving, vulnerable person she knew he was underneath, Daniel gradually stopped being defensive toward her. It took a while for him to respond, but people were shocked at how much he softened up. He still has a wry sense of humor, but his warmth and caring come through far more often now.

Roadblock: John sees his daughter as an angry person. When he and fourteen-year-old Jenny get into a fight, they tear each other apart verbally. They swear at each other and point out each other's faults. John feels terrible later, and worries because the fights escalate as Jenny gets older. He doesn't know what to do.

When we use anger to get our children to comply with our wishes, you can bet they will use anger back. This may not seem threatening when they're young, but it can be as they get older. Situations can quickly get out of control if we depend on power-oriented techniques with adolescents.

Being unable to control his own temper is a roadblock to John's approach to discipline. He inherited this tendency from his father, and Jenny is carrying on the family tradition. Both John and Jenny can break out of this destructive pattern but they need a counselor to do so. The problem has become too intense for them to handle themselves, and a counselor could put their relationship back on the right track.

Communication. We all talk about how important communication with teenagers is, but not many of us spend much time at it. We don't even expect them to communicate with us. Research shows that the average parent of a teenager spends 14½ minutes a day communicating with her child. Twelve minutes of that time is spent setting up schedules and working out routines. That leaves 2½ minutes a day for talking about feelings, settling conflicts, and just staying close.

Making an effort to communicate—setting up times for it, giving up other activities such as watching TV in order to do it—is more important than we may think. Communicating only helps our relationships, and studies show it is an important factor in preventing problems. Teenagers who report that they feel close to their parents and who feel they can communicate with them are more likely to postpone sexual activity and less likely to get involved with drugs than those who don't. In fact, communication with parents is a more important factor in preventing these problems than sex education or anti-drug education. It is more important because it offsets the negative aspects of peer pressure.

So learning to talk, and taking time to talk, isn't just fun— it's critical. Communicating at this new stage is no cinch. Young people want privacy. They don't want to share everything. But they will respond to a parent who isn't just trying to check up on them or find out all their secrets, a parent who really wants to talk.

Monica goes on walks with her daughter, Krissy. It started as a new physical fitness technique, because they both want to lose a little weight. Then Monica discovered that when they were away from the house things were different. It was natural to talk when they were walking. when they were away from the scene where they had to schedule everything and settle conflicts, they were more relaxed with each other. A new kind of sharing developed. Monica never said anything to Krissy, but she made sure that their walks were part of their routine.

Talking is easier when we do it regularly, casually, and don't bring up issues that make everything into a "big deal."

Roadblock: Fifteen-year-old Jason is going steady for the first time. He and his girlfriend spend all their spare time together and Jason's parents are a little concerned about the intensity of the relationship. They don't want Jason to get involved with sex prematurely and they feel that a strong one-to-one relationship makes this more likely than dating lots of girls. Sometimes they come home to find Jason entertaining his girlfriend in the bedroom with the door closed. A younger sibling has seen them kissing. Jason's parents would like to talk to him about these issues, but whenever they try to bring them up, Jason gets angry. They don't know what to do except rely on Jason's good sense.

Backing off because Jason seems uncomfortable is a roadblock for Jason's parents to communicating their guidelines. Jason needs to hear what his parents think about sexual relationships, what their feelings are about having a girl in his room, etc. He needs sensible limits. There should be rules about not having his girlfriend over when his parents aren't home, and he shouldn't be allowed to close the door to his room when she is visiting. These rules needn't be expressed in terms of distrusting him. They are only appropriate guidelines that any young person should follow.

To communicate effectively, Jason's parents are going to have to bear their temporary discomfort and even anger. But, if they pay attention to their relationship in other ways, communicating these new guidelines and ideas will not be so disruptive.

Good Judgment. If we expect our teenagers to have good judgment they are more apt to prove us right. We do need to supervise their activities and provide limits, but if we haven't learned this lesson we need to learn it now: Discipline is not a matter of controlling children. We can't force our adolescents to get good grades, make new friends, refrain from sexual activity, or become the people we would like them to be. When we see that our adolescents have their own personalities and approaches to life, we have an opportunity to learn something crucial. We have to provide sensible limits about curfews, chaperones at parties, driving and drinking, having friends over, dating, etc. But once we help them observe those rules, our expectations that they will have good judgment is one of the most important resources they have for becoming that way. That doesn't mean we should send them into inappropriate situations and say, "We trust you." It does imply that we aren't suspicious of our children nor do we expect negative behavior on their part.

Lots of Janelle's junior high friends have taken to smoking pot. Janelle tells her mother about it and Sandra is shocked, but never acts as if she is afraid that Janelle might take drugs too. When they talk about the subject Sandra expresses her concern for these other children and her appreciation of Janelle's good sense even when she is pressured by her friends to do something she doesn't want to.

Roadblock: When Melissa entered her freshman year of high school, boys started calling her for dates. Melissa's mother, Jane, was thrilled with her popularity and encouraged her daughter to go out whenever she wanted. Melissa herself felt overwhelmed—some of the boys were juniors and seniors with cars, and she wasn't ready for the sexual pressures she experienced with them—but she didn't want to disappoint her mother.

Jane's vicarious involvement in her daughter's popularity is a roadblock to using good judgment. At fourteen, Melissa isn't ready for dating in a one-to-one situation, especially with boys so much older than she is. Melissa needs protection. Her mother could help her by suggesting she postpone her involvement in dating—perhaps for a year. She could arrange for groups of boys and girls to come to the house and have a party or watch a video. Teenagers at this age need to get to know each other, and often don't have places to do this in enjoyable and appropriate ways. Jane also needs to establish sensible guidelines if Melissa does decide to date now, such as not going out alone with a boy in a car and not staying out late.

CONCLUSION

Good discipline builds on itself through the years. But facing roadblocks doesn't mean discipline has gone bad, or that we have failed as parents. If we never had to alter our perceptions or reevaluate our approaches, we wouldn't grow. As we mentioned earlier, no one knows automatically what to expect of a child. Assessing and reassessing our expectations is an integral part of discipline—in a sense it is the core. The point isn't to have the "right" expectations but to learn to reflect on the ways we see our children. Once we establish that process, we have the tools to gear our efforts toward the most beneficial results.

We don't establish expectations for our children in isolation. They develop in the context of other people, and are influenced by other children and adults. We need to be aware of what other parents feel and of the standards they set for their children. We need to communicate with our spouse or ex-spouse, our child's teacher or her babysitter, about their expectations. We may not come out with perfect unity, but the process of thinking together about expectations can help everyone's efforts.

5

Expectations for Ourselves

Now that we have explored the kinds of expectations that might be helpful for our children at different developmental stages, let's look at expectations we have for ourselves. After thinking about our disciplinary style and assessing our abilities to shape our children's behavior, what can we expect of ourselves realistically?

Should we be on top of every problem? Should we have the best-behaved kids on the block? Should we be able to advise our friends about discipline?

Many of today's parents have unrealistic expectations for themselves. And, when they can't fulfill these expectations, they feel inadequate. Parenting is often depicted as a kind of science in which people simply need to ingest a body of knowledge or keep abreast of the latest childrearing technology.

But that view of childrearing leaves out the most important part of the parenting process. It distracts us from our most crucial task: learning about ourselves and our children, and finding out what works for us.

If we approach discipline with an experimental attitude,

trying out what's right for us, we are more apt to have the essential energy for parenting. We will feel free to change our goals, drop ineffective approaches, or revamp our thinking as our children change and we gain new insights. That flexibility will also help us not to take unsuccessful approaches so personally. Recognizing that we can try many alternatives can keep us from feeling defeated.

When parents have unrealistic expectations for themselves, they can have a hard time learning and growing. Unreal expectations can form roadblocks to their growth, just as they do for children. We inherit expectations of parenting from adults we have known—mostly without it. We may not even be aware that we're expecting ourselves to get our children to obey without question, understand our thinking, or automatically sympathize with and appreciate us. If our parents operated under these assumptions we may continue that tradition with our own children. No one ever told us that these expectations were inappropriate; being aware of them can help us discover new satisfaction in our roles. Here are some questions that can help you approach parenting in a more realistic and satisfying fashion.

HAVE YOU GIVEN UP ON OMNIPOTENCE?

"I was so relieved when I realized that the goal of discipline wasn't to change my daughter's personality. She was always outspoken and not as sensitive to others as I thought she might be. I thought it was my job to teach her how to be a sensitive person. That's part of what I thought discipline was all about. But, as she grew older, I saw that *she* had to struggle with these issues. I also saw that she had other strengths. My job was to support her learning, not create her personality. Recognizing that she had her own personality took me off the hook."

Parents are often conditioned to think it's their job to shape their child's personality. Believing that we are responsible for everything our child becomes is a misinterpretation of modern psychology. The parent who tries to transform a boisterous preschooler into a sedate young man will find himself in an ongoing struggle. We can't *make* our children be reserved, extroverted, talented, smart, kind, or sensitive.

We can encourage and support positive qualities, but our children's personalities and capabilities are really their own. Our business is to help them form positive *habits,* not turn them into perfect people.

DO YOU NOTICE SMALL CHANGES?

> ADRIAN (mother of two): "My goals used to be having my children listen to me. I really worked on communicating and making sure my messages were clear. It took me a while to realize that my children were listening more. I was so concentrated on the process that I didn't know how to judge the results. When I saw the little ways that they were changing, I felt I could relax more. I saw that I *was* actually having an effect."

Many parents expect to be able to alter their child's misbehavior overnight, but change occurs in ways we may not see at first. When a child tries to hold her temper or study harder, no bells go off to signal us that she is actually responding positively to our guidance. We have to look for small changes if we want to see the fruits of our efforts.

One mother who had worked repeatedly with her daughter to convince her not to talk back had no idea that her efforts were making an impact. One day she asked her daughter to do an errand for her, and was upset because of the unpleasant look the girl gave her. She mentioned to her daughter that her frown displeased her and was surprised by the girl's explanation: "I was trying not to say anything back." It had never occurred to the mother that her daughter's frowns were a result of an effort to control her temper, and were positive steps toward change.

Keeping notes in a journal can help us to see changes we wouldn't otherwise have noticed. Parents are also helped by charting how often a behavior occurs over time. They can then see evidence of positive change no matter how gradual it is, or they can adjust their methods if they don't seem to have any effect.

When we look back at notes we have made, we get a sense that things aren't static. We are changing and so are our children. But if we expect ourselves to be superparents who can eradicate an undesirable behavior overnight, we will usually be disappointed and ineffective. Only if we expect change to be gradual and include steps backward as well as forward will we become better observers of change and more realistic.

Do You Expect Discipline to Stretch You?

GAY (mother of two): "I always had the idea that one should try to avoid conflict and that when stresses occurred between people it was a sign that something had gone wrong. That was why discipline was so unpleasant for me. Things would be going along nicely and suddenly my child and I were unhappy with each other. But gradually I began to see that having conflicts and feelings of discomfort while disciplining was absolutely normal. If we never had conflicts we wouldn't grow."

Discipline calls on us to stretch. Expecting ourselves always to be able to do it smoothly without anger, frustration, and even tears can leave us feeling inadequate. If we think we should automatically be able to discipline easily and effectively, we need to adjust our expectations.

It's hard to discipline. Each time we can do it without losing our tempers, feeling out of control, or tearing down our child's character we ought to give ourselves a pat on the back. Instead of focusing on an image of perfection—the calm, cool disciplinarian—we can benefit from celebrating our mild successes. How did we manage to follow through even when we were too tired to care if our child continued whatever he was doing? How many times today did we handle things matter-of-factly? When we remember our successes, we get a sense of the ways disciplining helps us to grow.

There are other satisfying and less challenging aspects of parenting that we all prefer. It's more fun to hold a child or play with him than to correct him. But because discipline is hard it calls up more of our resources.

We also need to remember that we can't rely on our children to give us a sense of our own success. They will protest when we oppose them, saying that we are unfair, nagging, or misunderstanding. But we don't have to let our children's reactions push our buttons or make us question our efforts. It is natural for them to project their own uncomfortable feelings onto us when they don't get what they want. They can't see how far we are stretching our capacity to handle them with kindness and insight. They shouldn't have to. But when *we* pay attention to our successes, it helps.

CAN YOU LAUGH AT YOURSELF AND YOUR PREDICAMENTS?

> MARY (mother of three): "One night my son was going through a hard time expressing his feelings to us. He was crying and we were all generally upset. We got him calmed down and my husband and I went in our bedroom and sat down for a few minutes together. However, as soon as we relaxed, my daughter rushed in and leapt onto the bed. She had just seen some pants that she wanted in *Seventeen* magazine. She had to know right now. Could she have them? Suddenly the whole role of being a parent seemed so ridiculous that I felt like laughing. There was no place to go in our house that would be free of problems."

Humor helps us to be more detached about the ups and downs of parenting. If we don't take ourselves too seriously or expect dramatic results, the whole process can be less overwhelming. Enjoying the humor of our situations also helps us to deal with our children. When we are accused of being unfair or insensitive we can joke about our lack of empathy and take the focus off a potential conflict.

Our humor should never be turned against our children, though. Using sarcasm to show how unimportant their problems are will only make them angry and alienated from us. But gentle humor that doesn't use anyone as a scapegoat can help everyone see that things aren't as dire as they seem.

Helene, the mother of two boys, eleven and three, has found humor a good way to sidestep unnecessary confrontations. She remembers the morning when Shelley, her three-year-old, was being grouchy and she could easily have had an argument with him. She started looking around the room as if she had lost something. "I wish that happy Shelly would come back," she said. "Where is he?" Drawn out of his emotions through laughter, Shelley couldn't help but respond. Humor can help us transcend the negative emotions associated with conflicts, too.

Do You Ignore the Stereotypes?

RACHEL (mother of two): "So even by the end of the first month—a milestone at which point many child development experts assured me in baby magazines and paperbacks that I would be on top of it with my child and tuned into his every need—I was completely floored. I was constantly tearful and floundering about with a baby whose cues I could not seem to read, despite my prenatal classes, and well-meaning advice of parents and sister-in-law."

Even though we all benefit from positive role models, we are also pulled down by the stereotypes of what we should be—false images of what parents are supposed to be like, what they're supposed to know, and how they're supposed to get their children to behave.

We benefit by reevaluating these images and accepting the reality of our own situations, which are more challenging than those the media portray. Perhaps words don't come as easily to us as they did to Robert Young on "Father Knows Best." Maybe we aren't as adept at knowing the best technique for helping a child to learn form his mistakes as the harmonious parents on "Leave It to Beaver." It's quite possible that active listening or assertive discipline techniques don't fit as easily into our routines as popular books promise.

But we can be reassured that *real* parents don't figure out all the solutions in a half hour. Sometimes insights are a long time coming and trial and error go on for weeks and months, or longer. It helps if we don't think our rate of learning has to conform to someone else's timetable.

CONCLUSION

When it comes right down to it, our goals as parents are not simply to be good "disciplinarians" but to be good parents— to love our children and to help them live healthy, productive lives. But, whether we want to or not, we must be disciplinarians, and feeling that we are doing a reasonable job in this role can make a big difference in our relationships with our children.

No one has all the answers to discipline. If we have some insights into how to work with our children, it's easier to keep problems in perspective and maintain our sense of humor. We hope this book has given you some ideas to try out right now in your life.

One specific thing we want you to take away from this book is an appreciation of your own efforts as a parent. Your children may never come back and thank you for trying to be a better disciplinarian, but we would like to. We can't think of a more practical contribution to a more harmonious and cooperative world.

Here is a final exercise to help you integrate what you have learned and to consolidate new goals.

WHAT ARE YOUR GOALS?

I want to work on _____.

Have you identified the areas of discipline you need to work on? Pick a difficult situation and go back through each area of discipline. How are you doing on thinking ahead? Motivating? Communicating? Following through? Working with others?

I will stand firm on _____.

What are the rules in your house? Are they clear to everyone concerned? Talk with your child about rules in a non-disciplining situation. What does he or she think needs to be changed? What new rules need to be developed?

Post the rules you come up with together or just write them down to refer to when necessary. Share new perceptions. Talk about goals for yourself and for each child. Plan new strategies for working together.

I need feedback from _____.

None of us can parent in isolation, so other adults are a valuable resource.

I want to think about _____.

Do your children ever pressure you in ways that make you give in without thinking? What issues would you like more time to think out? How can you program that time into your responses?

Think of ways to give yourself time out during decision-making. State clearly that you won't succumb to pressure, and consistently refuse to respond when your child exerts it.

I want to coordinate more effectively with my spouse on
_____.

Does your communication with a spouse (or another caregiver) ever tend to break down? Plan times when you can communicate outside the pressures of childrearing situations. Keep track of those times that seem most successful. How can you enhance them?

I want to think of new consequences for _____.

It's hard to follow through when you don't really think your efforts will work. Are there problem behaviors that your current methods don't seem to affect? Think of consequences that will impress your child, and motivate her to change her behavior.

I want consistently to follow through on _____.

Are there things that you tend to let slide when you are tired or your child is in a difficult mood? What are situations you need to remind yourself of to follow through on? Write them down or make a mental note of them.

I want to motivate my child to _____.

What are the positive behaviors you want to instill in your child? Explore the ways you could reinforce his own desire to behave in new ways. Do you praise him even for small efforts? Have you thought about rewards?

If you have a specific behavior in mind, plan out a system for motivating. Have a small reward every day when positive behavior occurs in a younger child (i.e., toilet training). Have a more long-range reward for an older child who is willing to work on a difficult habit.

I want communication to be _____.

Where does communication stand on your list of priorities? How can you schedule time for talking? With the help of others, we can develop new insights through mutual discussion and support. Whose opinion do you value? Sometimes it helps to make notes for our child's pediatrician, teacher, or babysitter. What information do we need from them to expand our own understanding? How do their views on a particular problem compare with ours? We may not always agree, but discussions help us clarify our thinking.

Additional Reading

Baumrind, Diane. "Parental Control and Parental Love," *Children:* pp. 230–235, Vol. 12, No. 6, November–December 1965, U.S. Department of Health, Education, and Welfare, Children's Bureau.

————. "Parental Disciplinary Patterns and Social Competence in Children," *Youth and Society,* Vol. 9, No. 3, March 1978, Sage Publication.

Bayard, Jean, Ph.D., and Robert Bayard, Ph.D. *How to Deal with Your Acting Up Teenager: Practical Self-Help for Desperate Parents.* San Jose, CA: The Accord Press, 1981.

Buntman, Peter H., and Eleanor M. Saris. *How to Live with Your Teenager: A Survivor's Handbook for Parents.* Pasadena, CA: Birch Tree Press, 1979.

Coopersmith, Stanley. *Antecedents of Self-Esteem.* San Francisco: W.H. Freeman & Co., 1967.

Dreikurs, Rudolf, and Vicki Soltz. *Children: The Challenge.* New York: Hawthorn Books, 1964.

Faber, Adelle, and Elaine Mazlish. *Liberated Parents, Liberated Children.* New York: Avon Books, 1975.

Fornaciari, Suzanne. *How to Talk to Kids About Drugs.* Bethesda, MD: Potomac Press, 1980.

Ginott, Haim. *Between Parent and Child.* New York: Avon Books, 1956.

Glenn, H. Stephen. *Strengthening the Family.* Bethesda, MD: Potomac Press, 1981.

Gordon, Thomas. *P.E.T.—Parent Effectiveness Training.* New York: Peter H. Wyden, 1970.

National Institute of Mental Health. *Families Today.* Washington, DC: U.S. Government Printing Office, 1977.

Index